BETTER LETTERS

A Guide to Proper Letter Writing

Bernard Smith

B T BATSFORD LTD
LONDON

For Paul, Elaine, and Cathryn

ACKNOWLEDGMENTS

The lines from 'Night Mail' quoted in the introduction are reprinted by permission of Faber & Faber Ltd from *Collected Poems* by W.H Auden. The drawings are by Linda Sandey.

Text © Bernard Smith 1985
Illustrations © B.T. Batsford Ltd 1985
First published 1985

ISBN 0 7134 4699 4

Filmset by
Progress Filmsetting Ltd

Printed in Great Britain
by Butler & Tanner Ltd
Frome, Somerset
for the publishers
B.T. Batsford Ltd
4 Fitzhardinge Street
London W1H 0AH

CONTENTS

INTRODUCTION

Letters of thanks, letters from banks,
  Letters of joy from girl and boy,
Receipted bills and invitations,
  To inspect new stock or to visit relations,
And applications for situations,
  And timid lovers' declarations,
And gossip, gossip from all the nations.
                    W.H. Auden: 'Night Mail'

Letter writing is the art of everyman. Needing no skill other than that of literacy, it enables people from all walks of life and of all ages to communicate with those around them—and even with future generations.

In an era of instant access, of messages sped round the world by satellite, it might be thought that letters are becoming redundant. We feel, possibly, that they will soon be little more than nostalgic reminders of days when people had more time to spare, when they were...well, perhaps not quite so efficient and modern as we like to think we are now. And yet, precisely because of this growth in fast communication, more and more people are coming to appreciate the importance and, often, the sheer joy of the written word.

You can't usually secure a new job by telephone. How many of us are brave enough to ring through a complaint, confident in our ability to speak the right words off the cuff to someone who seems to have all the answers? And what about the long-distance call when the person you're ringing can't or won't be reached? To a lover a letter can be a constant reminder of a distant partner; to the lonely or bereaved it becomes a source of consolation or a physical link with days now past. In all those circumstances, and many others, a letter gives us time to think, presenting our thoughts in a tangible and often more valued form.

As with all arts, styles differ; what is right for one sort of letter may be wrong for another. But you don't have to be 'good with words', nor need you worry about knowing all the formalities once considered so important. The rules are comparatively few and easily learned, and in this book I shall explain them simply and show you how to write letters that will achieve the results you want. Equally important, I want to demonstrate that letter writing can be fun.

Before we begin, however, permit me a word of explanation to those who, like myself, believe in the total equality of the sexes. You will notice that, throughout the book, when writing generally, I have used the words 'he', 'him', and 'his'. I have tried all the expressions I can think of which would avoid charges of my being biased, and feel that these are the only ones in their context which make easy reading. So I ask all lady readers to do the personable thing and forgive any apparent but unintended discourtesy.

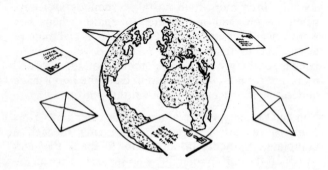

Chapter One
GENERAL CONSIDERATIONS

Used correctly, words can do most things. They can obtain orders, make excuses, settle strikes—and start them; they can cajole your bank manager or the building society into giving you a loan; they can irritate, delight or console. They can persuade someone to go to dinner with you or to marry you...and all stages in between. They can end domestic squabbles or begin wars. And for you to do all of these—or anything else—with a letter, you need remember only two things: the first is to have always before you a clear picture of why you are writing; and the second is for you never to forget the effect your words will have on the recipient.

Before you begin to write, ask yourself what you hope to achieve by your letter. What results do you want? If the washing machine you've just bought finishes the weekly laundry by dumping soapy water all over the floor, a refinement you hadn't envisaged when you bought it, you might reasonably feel constrained to write to the store and ask what they propose to do about the problem. But hold hard with the vitriol; calm down for a moment, and think. Do you want to give the store manager a piece of your mind, beat him around the ears with your ballpoint, and annoy him? Or would you prefer him to repair your washing machine, say what a kind, understanding customer you are, and—who knows?—perhaps even throw in a little something for your trouble? You can have either result, but not both...and the one you get will depend on the way you write your letter. When you go fishing you bait

7

your hook with what the fish likes, not what you find tasty. That is why it is important to know what you want when you sit down to write, and it brings us to the second important point.

Remember always to think of the effect your letter is going to have on the person to whom you're writing. Ask yourself if you would *speak* to him or her like that. It's surprising how brave—and sometimes how down-right rude—we can become when sheltering behind a pen or a typewriter. Try to put yourself in his position, and visualize your own reaction to receiving such a letter. Make it easy for him to do what you want...and he won't find it easy if he's made to feel angry or foolish.

The amount of time you spend in preparation before beginning to write depends to a large extent on the sort of letter you are going to send. The following checklist will help you make sure you have not overlooked anything and that you are covering everything in the best possible order.

1 What am I writing about? What results do I want this letter to produce?

2 Have I all the information I need—*before* I begin writing?

3 What will interest my correspondent in the subject of my letter? How can I seize and hold his attention? As a general principle, you may be sure that anything which makes him feel good or appreciated will capture anyone's attention at once, and goes a long way towards making him willing to do what you want.

4 How much does my correspondent already know about the subject of my letter? Don't waste his time and your own by going over ground with which you're both familiar, although vows of undying love will, I dare say, stand repeating to everyone's advantage. If you need, however, to sketch in the background to your subject, do so early in the letter, but make sure you do it, or the other person is going to wonder what you are writing about.

Chapter Two
MATERIALS, LAYOUT, AND CONSTRUCTION

Materials

The appearance of a person's letter has, in many ways, the same effect as has the way he dresses. Just as you would be unlikely to wear casual clothes to an interview for a job, so you would be wise to avoid the use of floral-decorated notepaper for business letters. And in the same way as you wouldn't visit friends in the outfit you wear for servicing the car, you would not usually write them letters written on unused pages torn from the end of a school exercise book. Apart from being discourteous, it can have practical disadvantages. I remember a letter I once received dealing with an important legal matter: written almost illegibly in smudged ballpoint ink on a page torn from a spiral shorthand notebook, it spoke volumes about the sender and gave me a valuable guide to the best course of action to follow.

Notepaper is available in just about any colour you want, if you're prepared to look hard enough, and the old saying that white was the only paper in good taste has long since been outmoded. But if your heart is set on a tinted paper, it is as well to remember that dark backgrounds don't make for easily-read writing, so stay with pastel shades; pale blue is an attractive colour, as is the maize tint that some companies are turning to for their letterheads.

Business letters are generally safest written on a good quality white paper, and if you are typing them you will find that the international A4 size and perhaps the smaller A5 are the best to keep by you. Some countries, such as the United States of America, use paper whose sizes vary slightly from these, but this is unlikely to present problems unless you write for their Press and find yourself sending their editors manuscripts which won't fit into the files.

As a general rule, it is considered most courteous to write on only one side of the paper, although nowadays many people relax this rule when writing personal letters, especially if they have a lot to say—perhaps one of the less immediately apparent social effects of increasing postal charges. Business correspondence, however, should always be confined to one side of each sheet.

When sending letters by air mail, you will find it least expensive if you use lightweight stationery, and good quality material will allow you to write on both sides of the paper without the ink soaking right through. As economical a way as any is to use the *air letter forms*, already stamped, available from all post offices. These have the added advantage, if you are short of news, of limited space, thus enabling you with a clear conscience to sign off comparatively early.

Always use good quality *envelopes*, sufficiently opaque to conceal what you have written. They should match your paper in both style and size, so that you are able to fold your letters neatly. That unused greetings card envelope might appear tempting, but I can tell you from experience that your carefully written and folded letter always proves to be a few millimetres too wide to go in without an extra fold along the edge...or is so undersized as to be just as much of a giveaway.

Layout and Construction

Your Address

The first thing that should appear on any letter you write is your address; this is most often, and usually best, placed on the right half of the page. Don't assume that your correspondent will know it, even if you've been writing to him for years; his memory mightn't be as good as yours, and he might have lost his address book. But it is in any event good manners to save him the trouble of having to look up the information or, worse, of having to wonder who on earth is writing to him. This advice doesn't apply, of course, if your name happens to be A. Wellwisher and you write the sort of letters that are full of interesting information about the other person's spouse.

Although the only part common to all your letters, and so presumably the easiest, it helps to keep things neat if you remember one or two simple rules about how to set out your address. These are best explained with the help of a few examples.

(a) 9 Doctors Road
CUTTINGHAM
Herts.
AL1 0FF

(b) "Dreaming Spires"
7a Gasworks Street
Pepperley
BIRMINGHAM
BM7 2BA

(c) "Llamessuc"
Traethygongl
LYFERDWC
Gwynedd
LL99 0IC

11

These examples cover, in one form or another, most types of address common in the United Kingdom, and will give a good guide to any modification that might be needed. Overseas, customs vary from country to country, but you should be able easily to adapt the layout to suit local requirements. The substitution of state for county would produce, say, the Australian arrangement; replace postcode with zip code, and United States usage is covered. And, of course, if you're sending your letters abroad, use one more line at the end to show, in capitals, the name of your country.

Nowadays, it is usual not to include punctuation in the address except in some forms of abbreviation (see page 44), but, if you prefer, you may use a comma at the end of each line other than the last; this takes a full stop.

Notice, too, the correct way to write the name of your *post town* and your *postcode*. Both should appear clearly in capitals. Never join postcode characters together, and don't use punctuation of any sort here. Leave a clear space, equivalent to one or two characters, between the two parts of the code.

Leave a blank line below your address and then, immediately underneath it, write the *date*. Modern practice is to set it out thus: 12 August 1984. This avoids any possibility of confusion, such as might arise if you place the month before the day. For the same reasons, it is best not to use the abbreviated form 12.8.84; some countries, notably the United States of America, follow the convention of quoting the month before the day when using all numbers, and there could be a real chance of mistaking 12 August for 8 December.

Unless you are using a business or printed personal letterhead—which should, if correctly designed, ensure that your letters are always properly headed—the best place for your *telephone number*, if you have one, is normally at the left of the page and level with the first line of your address. It helps, too, if you include the area dialling code in brackets between the name of the exchange and the number. The following example shows the effect to aim for:

Anytown (0234) 9876

6 Shaldon Road
ANYTOWN
Devon
AY5 6SR

21 June 1984

Mr John Smith
Manager
National Westminster Bank plc
51 High Street
ANYTOWN
AY1 2BD

Dear Mr Smith,
        Thank you for your letter of 18 June...etc.

Your Correspondent's Address

You will have noticed one or two other details in these few lines, perhaps most obviously that I've included the name and address of the recipient. This is not required in a personal letter, but is good practice in all business correspondence. In some companies mail is opened at a central point before being passed to the person concerned, and the envelopes are discarded, so it is important that the letter itself carries clear instructions for whom it is intended. And, since it is not unknown for mail to be wrongly delivered, the inclusion of his full address is a sensible precaution.

Construction

Your first aim when writing a letter is to *convey information*, and you will do this much more clearly if you make it easy for the other person to read. Typewritten lines don't often overlap, but it is worth taking care to ensure that handwriting is not cramped so closely as to run the lines into each other. And, unless you're really down to your last sheet of paper and the shops are shut, leave a reasonable margin all round the text. 2 to 2.5 cm. (¾ to 1 in.) is usually about right, although the arrangement of printed letter-headings may require you to alter this slightly in order to align your writing neatly with the printing.

Indent the first line of each paragraph; in other words, begin it about 2 cm. (¾ in.) further to the right than the other lines. Some companies prefer not to indent first lines in their business letters, and if yours is one such, then letters you write for them had best conform. But indentation helps identify clearly where each new paragraph begins, and most authorities agree that this is sounder practice, in addition to being a neater presentation. In any event, however, always leave a blank line between paragraphs; this avoids confusing facts which might not have any relation to each other, and, again, makes for a better looking and more easily understood letter.

While the finer points of English grammar and usage are beyond the scope of this book, some readers might welcome a little guidance on what constitutes sentences and paragraphs.

The first, and most important, advice is *don't worry*. A sentence usually consists of one complete thought or statement; when you've come to the end of it, put in a full stop, and begin the next sentence with a capital letter. One description of a paragraph is a collection of sentences dealing with the same subject, and to some extent this is true. But it can often be said that an entire letter deals with only one subject; remember the washing machine? In such a case, keep together in paragraphs those sentences dealing with one aspect of the matter: the washing machine cleans the clothes nicely, and you're very pleased about that. It also washes your feet, the walls, and the floor, and you're less keen on that part of its performance. You're sure the store is as concerned about it as you are and is anxious to maintain its excellent reputation for after-sales service, so you will be pleased to hear when they will be round to put things right.

Each of my sentences about the washday saga is a summary of what you might deal with in a paragraph, and you'll rarely find it necessary to exceed fifteen lines in any. Indeed, it's perfectly possible to have a one-line paragraph, and if you've said all you have to say about a subject in one short sentence, then end your paragraph right there and start a new one on the next line. Simple, isn't it?

Try to make your letter *well-written*. That doesn't mean you need a degree in English, or even that your standard in the subject at school should have been good enough to earn you the privilege of handing out the pencils. Use simple, straightforward words, short sentences and concise paragraphs, and the chances are that your letter will be easy to read and to understand. Long, complex sentences are rarely so easy, and present a real danger of obscuring or even altering completely the meaning of what you want to say. What's more, they are almost always boring.

Ensure that spelling, punctuation, and grammar are as correct as possible, especially in business letters. There is more flexibility in personal letters, of course, but the more nearly correct a business one is the more favourably it is likely to be received; and where any correspondence is legally binding, it is safest to make quite sure, even to the extent of taking advice, that your letter means what it should.

A nurse wrote to her health authority to complain about her supervisor at the centre where they both worked. Her letter said: 'I have come to the opinion that Mrs Blank is out to make my life hell, so I give in my notice.' Mark that comma. What the nurse had *meant* to say was that her supervisor had been harassing her with the intention of making her leave her job. But what she *wrote* was that, because of the supervisor's persecution, she was quitting; and it came as a painful surprise when, at the end of the month, she found her resignation had been accepted and that she was out of work.

15

Don't use two or more words when one will do. You don't, for example, 'meet up with' someone; you 'meet' them. And use short words rather than long ones whenever you can; they are generally more effective and are less likely to be misunderstood. Never use any word unless you're absolutely sure of its meaning; there's not much point in impressing yourself and giving the other person the wrong idea. The lady who wrote to the Department of Health and Social Security: 'Please send my money at once, as I have fallen into errors with the landlord,' might have been safer had she been satisfied with falling behind with her rent.

Avoid needless words. If the letter is an important one, it would be as well to write a rough draft first so that you can make any necessary alterations before tackling the real thing. Go through it carefully, and eliminate everything that does not help towards obtaining the result you want. Take care not to pad your letter with unnecessary details just to make it look longer and more impressive: longer it will be, impressive it won't. And finally, when you want to say something make sure you've said it; check what you have written, and make sure that the impression it gives is the one you intended. If it isn't, now is the time to put things right, not after your correspondent has read it and reacted in the very way you didn't want.

Addressing the Envelope

Having taken a great deal of care over your letter, you naturally want it to arrive safely, but it won't do so unless you take similar care when addressing the envelope. The men and women of the Post Office who sort and deliver our mail are usually a canny lot, but they're only human, and if you don't make it clear where you want your letter sent you can't blame them if it goes astray.

I once received a letter, posted five days earlier in the outback of Australia, bearing nothing more than my name, the county, and the correct postcode. Just that. No town. Not even 'United Kingdom'. Whether it reached me by courtesy of Aboriginal magic or the exercise of commendable initiative by several people I'll never know; I was grateful that it arrived at all. But it's unwise to count on such service all the time: the same post brought a correctly-addressed letter which had taken six days to travel by first-class mail the 250 miles from London. So the moral clearly is to take no chances.

The first thing to remember is that you're going to have to stick a stamp on the envelope, and that the Post Office expect it to be in the top right-hand corner. They do this for the good reason that the automatic machinery which cancels the stamp expects it to be there and not, as one wag I know once placed it, in the centre of the envelope. (A letter of complaint from the Post Office to him about this practice produced a reply, again stamped centrally, which ran: *'Hi diddle diddle, the stamp's in the middle'.*)

To deface stamps which are placed rather less out of position, the postmark normally extends well across the top of the envelope, so make sure you put the first line of the address safely out of range. About one third of the way down is about right. Then just write the name and address in the same way as you write your own address at the beginning of the letter; you'll remember we dealt with that earlier in this chapter. You can stagger the address if you wish, or you might prefer the modern business practice of beginning each line directly below that above.

Unless the letter is intended for abroad—in which case the name of the country goes last—the postcode should always be the last item in an address, preferably on a line by itself. Don't underline it, use no punctuation, and leave a space of one or two characters' width between the two parts. If you're unable to give it a line to itself place it to the right of the last line of the address, with a clear space of between two and six characters in front of it.

Any reference number you might wish to include on

the envelope should be kept well away from the postcode, above and to the left of the name and address—unless, of course, you are of a wicked turn of mind and want to make things difficult for the Post Office.

A good idea, and one gaining increasing acceptance, is to write your own name and address, preceded by the word 'from', on the back flap of the envelope. This ensures that if, for any reason, your letter cannot be delivered it will be returned to you unopened. A final word of advice relates especially to business letters. Unless the contents of your letter are strictly confidential or personal, it is best not to state this on the envelope. Nor is it always wise, unless you are reasonably sure he will be there, to address the envelope to an officer of the company specifically by name. There is nothing wrong in doing either of these things, of course, if you know to whom you are writing and intend your letter for his eyes only. But it's as well to check that he is there, or it might arrive just after he has gone away for a month, and could then remain unopened until his return.

Having dealt here with the proper manner of addressing our envelope, in the next chapters we shall look at the correct ways to address our correspondents.

Chapter Three
STARTING AND FINISHING YOUR LETTER

Let's get two long words out of the way at once. The first, 'salutation', is the formal name for the beginning of the letter, the 'Dear...' part. The 'valediction' is the way in which you sign off: 'Yours disgustedly' and the like. I mention them for the record and because some readers might look for them in the index; but I try to follow my own advice, so let's refer to these parts of our letters by more easily-understood names. How about starting and finishing, or beginning and ending?

Starting the Letter

Clearly, the way in which you begin a letter depends on the person to whom you're writing. Just as you wouldn't usually walk up to your diocesan bishop, slap him on the back, and say, 'Good to see you, Holy Joe', so it's unlikely that you would write to him in the same way as you would to an old army mate—even if that's what he was. You begin, and end, a letter in a way appropriate to the person who is going to receive it, and your first decision, then, must be whether to adopt a social or formal mode of address.

'*Dear Sir*' or '*Dear Madam*' is the formal, correct, and safest way to begin when you are writing to a complete stranger of whom you know little. 'Dear' as used here is nothing more than a term of courtesy and is standard form at all levels of correspondence. The chances are that when your local Inspector of Taxes writes to you he will start his letter thus; don't assume that he feels undue affection towards you. Indeed, if he begins with plain '*Sir*' or '*Madam*', you can be sure that affection is the last thing in his mind; these are the very formal styles reserved for those occasions when it is important that the contents of the letter be regarded as impersonal and authoritative in the extreme.

You may find that your first letter, though written in a formal style, receives a reply couched in more social terms. How you follow this up depends on how you want the relationship to develop, but it's clear that your correspondent is trying to be friendly, and, unless you have good reasons for keeping him at arm's length, it helps to respond in kind.

So your next letter might begin '*Dear Mr Jones*', and this is how you would usually open when writing to people whose names you know and with whom you feel able to be on friendly but not intimate terms. In passing, I have to say that my own experience of writing to Her Majesty's Inspectors of Taxes has yet to produce a reply headed with anything other than 'Dear Sir', no matter how friendly I strive to be.

When you are on friendly terms with the other person but do not feel justified in using his first name, the more informal style of inserting 'My' before 'Dear' is perhaps warranted. So a letter to your children's head teacher might begin '*My dear Miss Marshall*' if you and she know each other well because of, say, serving together on the local community council.

When two male correspondents are well acquainted and are equal in age and social importance, they will sometimes adopt the form '*Dear Johnson*'. This style is also occasionally used when one is writing to a younger man in a more junior position, but my own preference in such cases is for the more courteous and equally correct '*Dear Mr Johnson*'. A good rule to remember is that the use of courtesy does not run the risk of unwittingly offending anyone.

The American practice of using both first name and surname is sometimes adopted in Britain and other parts of the English-speaking world. The idea behind this is that it falls half-way in formality between the use of first name and of surname. Thus we have letters beginning *'Dear Paul Richardson'*. Some people consider the form useful in the business world, but others, myself included, do not like it, feeling it to be stilted, and unsuitable on any grounds. One might approach a person and say: 'How are you today, Paul?', or 'Good morning, Mrs Robinson', or 'It's good to see you, Ms Brown'; but 'Nice weather we're having, John Smith' sounds and is awkward. And so, I feel, is its use at the beginning of a letter.

Beginning personal correspondence is much easier, and here again a little thought will show you the right words to use. While *'Dear…'* is always a safe beginning, there will be times when you want to start in a more intimate or affectionate way. Then such openings as *'My dear Tom'* or perhaps *'Dearest Anne'* are perfectly in order. It is true to say that when you write such letters you won't go wrong if you begin in much the same words as you would were you speaking to the other person face to face. And that in itself suggests a caution.

Although actions for breach of promise are largely things of the past, it is still worth remembering that sentiments committed to writing tend to carry more weight than do the same thoughts whispered at a time when the blood is running hot. So it is important, when writing to someone of the opposite sex who just might misunderstand your feelings, that you be especially careful not to convey too strong a sense of affection. Where *'My dear Jo'* would normally be a perfectly satisfactory way of starting a letter to a close friend, to use that form in such circumstances could well create an embarrassing situation. And getting out of it will almost certainly cause a great deal of pain and perhaps the loss of a good friend.

Of course, if you are writing to someone of whom you are genuinely fond or lust after passionately, there are no real limits to the expressions you can use to begin

21

the outpourings of your soul. What's more, you won't need me to tell you what to say. *'Darling Mabel'* is but the starting point; you can supply your own superlatives and embellishments as appropriate to the occasion and relationship. The same principles apply here as in all letter writing: take your time, think of the effect your words will create...and if you have second thoughts, don't hesitate to scrap the letter and start again. That's the beauty of writing: you can consider, and if necessary recall, your first outburst with no harm done.

Using whichever of the foregoing openings is suitable, you should be able to begin most of your letters. But, democracy being what it is, from time to time we may find ourselves writing to people whose positions or occupations require a more elaborate approach. Although modern custom tends even in such cases towards less rigidity, some people still prefer to use the very formal and traditional styles. As a guide to those readers who do, these are listed in the next chapter. It is, however, fairly safe to assume that no letter begun politely and with normal formality would now be looked on less favourably than one where every nicety of protocol has been strictly observed.

Finishing the Letter

As with the opening, correspondence with especially close friends or members of one's family poses no problems. Traditionally, letters to parents, children, brothers, and sisters would end *'Your loving (or affectionate) son/mother'*, or whatever is appropriate. These endings are fine and would never cause offence, but I believe that, while still retaining a proper degree of formality in business correspondence, there is much to be said for the exercise of a little common sense with personal letters. Having begun with 'My dear Dad', it's hardly necessary for you to remind him at the end that you're still his daughter. So *'With all my love, Mary'*, or *'Yours lovingly, Jennie'* would seem much more natural a way to sign off and in no way disrespectful.

The same care in closing letters to friends of the opposite sex is required as in opening them. Between husband and wife, or lovers, the ending should never present any difficulties. Your relationship will already be such that the right expressions of affection will arise spontaneously, and you will employ the terms of endearment you use when together. 'Your own Fatso' can convey just as much love as can 'With all my heart, darling' between those for whom it is an intimate and teasing nickname.

A little more thought is required, though, when signing off a letter to someone who is not an intimate friend but who would like to become one. 'Yours with love' is likely to be regarded as nothing more than a friendly good-bye in metropolitan London, but might be taken very much at face value in, say, the Welsh hills, and you could find yourself with an unexpected response. Once more, let common sense be your guide, and if you're in doubt choose the safer alternative.

The way in which you end letters to friends or to business associates depends to some extent on how you begin them. You will be pleased to learn that the choice of 'standard' wording is comparatively limited. Indeed, with *'Yours sincerely'*, *'Yours faithfully'*, and *'Yours truly'*, you can close almost any letter. And the rules for applying these three forms are simple.

If you start 'Dear Francis' or 'Dear Mrs Anderson' (in other words, if you know them well enough to use their name) the usual and correct ending is *'Yours sincerely'* or *'Yours very sincerely'*. American practice sometimes differs slightly by employing just *'Sincerely'*.

More formal business letters—those starting with 'Dear Sir', 'Dear Madam', or the awe-inspiring 'Sir'—are ended with *'Yours faithfully'* or *'Yours truly'*. There is a fine distinction between these two forms in that *faithfully* is used for ordinary business correspondence, and *truly* (or *very truly*) when you don't know the recipient of the letter and the subject is not strictly a matter of business. This is a slightly less distant form of closing than 'Yours faithfully' and could be used, say, when writing to a local councillor, or perhaps a school.

You might think that the act of signing one's name at the end of a letter poses no problems. And it doesn't, as long as your writing is legible and you're known to your correspondent. Perhaps, however, like many people, you have a signature decipherable only by yourself and the Almighty; in that case, you will be helpful and will avoid any possible confusion and embarrassment if, beneath the signature, you make clear who and what you are. Indeed, such practice is standard in business correspondence.

All that is required is for you to type—or, if you are writing by hand, print in block capitals—the form of your name by which your correspondent can reply to you: 'J. D. Brown' or 'John Brown'. It is generally assumed that if a name is shown as initials and surname, it belongs to a man, so clearly it is best for ladies to indicate how they wish to be addressed if the point is important to them. This is done by following your typed or printed name by brackets containing the required information, thus: 'J. D. Brown (Miss)', 'J. D. Brown (Ms)', or 'Joan Brown (Mrs)'.

If you don't make your name and status clear, you have only yourself to blame for the way your correspondent interprets your signature. I recently received a communication (it couldn't be dignified by being called a letter) bearing, where the signature should have been, a mark apparently made by an inebriated earwig that had omitted to wipe its feet. Unfortunately, the earwig required a reply, and, since it hadn't indicated where in the organization it was employed, I spent several minutes before deciding that its name could only be P. Pnhum Mu/reen. The name looked odd on the envelope, it's true, but my crystal ball was at the cleaners, and this was the best I could come up with.

Depending on your skill with words and the purpose of your message, there is scope for a degree of originality in the way you finish your letter, but you need to be very sure of what you are doing. For instance, I once ended a letter of complaint to the Post Office 'Yours frankly', while a fruit importer received a note couched in rather hurt terms and signed 'Yours unapplely'. Both received immediate and sympathetic attention, not least because their complaints were voiced in a friendly and humorous way. Had a more conventional and serious approach been adopted, the letters would have ended 'Yours faithfully'. Here again, the standard endings are tried, trusted, and always safe.

If, however, you prefer a more formal—or even a very formal—closing for that very special letter, one of the following examples will almost certainly be suitable, depending on circumstances. Just which one you need can be determined by referring to the summary of Titles and Forms of Address in the following chapter.

Formal

I remain (*or* I am),
Sir / Madam / Reverend Sir / Mr Chairman / Mr President / Mr Mayor / My Lord Mayor / Your Excellency/Right Reverend Sir/Most Reverend Sir/ Your Grace, etc.

Very Formal

What follows is, to put it mildly, involved. But take heart; you don't really need to go to such lengths nowadays. And if you think these forms are complicated, you need only look at the ones which were once in fashion to make you feel better. Then there was an elaborate scale of 'Most devoted and most obedient', 'Most obedient', 'Most humble and devoted', 'Most humble and obedient', and so on. Correspondents meriting somewhat less abject submission were addressed as above but with the word '*most*' omitted.

Dukes and Duchesses

I have the honour to be (*or* to remain),
My Lord Duke (*or* Madam),
Your Grace's obedient servant,

Other Peers, and Those Styled Lord
  I have the honour to be (*or* to remain),
    My Lord,
      Your Lordship's obedient servant,

Other Peeresses, and Those Styled Lady
  I have the honour to be (*or* to remain),
    Madam,
      Your Ladyship's obedient servant,

Baronets, Knights and Esquires (including Privy Counsellors and Ministers of the Crown)
  I have the honour to be (*or* to remain),
    Sir,
      Your obedient servant,
(NB This does not apply when 'Esquire' or 'Esq.' is used as an alternative to 'Mr'. See the list of titles and forms of address which follows.)

Untitled Ladies
  I have the honour to be (*or* to remain),
    Madam,
      Your obedient servant,

Archbishops
  I have the honour to be (*or* to remain),
    Your Grace (*or* My Lord Archbishop),
      Your Grace's obedient servant,

Bishops
  I have the honour to be (*or* to remain),
    My Lord Bishop (*or* Right Reverend Sir),
      Your Lordship's obedient servant,

Other Appointments
As for *Baronets, Knights and Esquires* or *Untitled Ladies* (above), but with the appropriate alteration in the second line, e.g. Reverend Sir, Mr Dean (or Very Reverend Sir), Mr (or Madam) President, Mr (or Madam) Chairman. The use of 'Chairwoman' or 'Chairperson' would, I suggest, sound awkward; the suffix '-*man*', is used here with its generic, rather than sexual, meaning.

Chapter Four
TITLES AND FORMS OF ADDRESS

Royalty

The Sovereign

Unless you are a personal friend of Her Majesty, it is best not to write directly to her. She spends a lot of time away from home on affairs of State and is always kept busy by an already large daily postbag from all manner of official sources. So if you decide to write, your letter will in any event be intercepted by her staff. The correct thing to do is to address your communication to 'The Private Secretary to Her Majesty The Queen'.

You may approach your subject by suggesting that 'It may interest Her Majesty to learn that...etc.' or ask that 'Her Majesty's attention be directed to..'; or you can ask him to 'submit for Her Majesty's approval (or consideration)...' and so on.

Don't address your first letter to the Private Secretary by name; begin it 'Dear Sir' followed by the usual 'Yours faithfully' close; when he replies, however, all subsequent correspondence should be directed personally to him. The first reference to The Queen should be as 'Her Majesty', and all subsequent ones as 'The Queen'. Where you would normally write 'She' and 'Hers', substitute 'Her Majesty', and 'Her Majesty's'.

Should you be one of The Queen's friends and writing to her directly, the following is the form to use:

27

Beginning of Letter
  Madam,
  With my humble duty,

Ending of Letter
  I have the honour to remain (*or* to be),
    Madam,
      Your Majesty's most humble and obedient servant,

If you choose to quarrel with the 'obedient' part here, please don't try to enlist my support, I prefer my present address to the Tower of London. And, since you are a friend of The Queen, you'll know, won't you, that in the body of your letter you should insert 'Her Majesty' and 'Her Majesty's' where 'You' and 'Yours' would normally appear?

Other Members of the Royal Family

As with letters to The Queen, unless you are known personally to the Prince, Princess, Duke, etc. to whom you're writing, the correct form in the first instance is to address your message to the Equerry, Lady in Waiting, or Private Secretary of the person concerned.

Again, you will begin 'Dear Sir' or 'Dear Madam', closing with the standard 'Yours faithfully'. In the body of your letter, the first reference to the member of the Royal Family should be 'His (*or* Her) Royal Highness' or 'His (*or* Her) Grace' as appropriate. Subsequent ones are expressed as 'Prince...', 'The Duke of...', and so on. Discreet use of 'His Royal Highness' and 'His Royal Highness's' for 'Him' and 'His', etc. should be made when possible, but avoid the confusion which too liberal a sprinkling of these terms would create.

* * * *

In the forms of address which follow, the choice of formal or social style is left to the writer's discretion and will naturally depend on the purpose of the letter. If, for example, you were asking a peer not known personally to you to accept a post on a board of

directors, it would be courtesy to adopt the formal style. On the other hand, once he is serving with you on the board and you want to canvass his support in a forthcoming meeting, the social terms would be appropriate.

Duke
Beginning of Letter
Formal   My Lord Duke
Social   Dear Duke (*or*, if your acquaintanceship is slight, Dear Duke of Marlborough)

Ending of Letter
Formal   Yours faithfully
Social   Yours sincerely

Envelope
Formal   His Grace the Duke of Marlborough
Social The Duke of Marlborough

I'm reliably informed that a few Dukes still prefer to be called 'His Grace', so to avoid possible offence, however slight, it might be advisable always to retain the formal usage.

Duchess
Beginning of Letter
Formal   Madam *or* Dear Madam
Social   Dear Duchess (*or*, if you know her only slightly, Dear Duchess of Devonshire)

Ending of Letter
Formal   Yours faithfully
Social   Yours sincerely

Envelope
Formal   Her Grace the Duchess of Devonshire
Social   The Duchess of Devonshire

Marquess, Earl, Viscount and Baron
In conversation, peers of all the above grades are referred to simply as 'Lord...', the dots here standing for the name of the peerage. So the Earl of Huntingdon

would be addressed in person as 'Lord Huntingdon'. Unless it has for some reason to be specifically mentioned, the use of the exact rank in speech is usually incorrect. When writing to them, however, while the opening and closing of the letter is the same for all, it is customary to give their full rank on the envelope.

Beginning of Letter
Formal   My Lord
Social   Dear Lord Derby

Ending of Letter
Formal   Yours faithfully
Social   Yours sincerely

Envelope
Formal   The Most Hon. the Marquess of Exeter
          The Rt Hon. the Earl of Lichfield
          The Rt Hon. the Viscount Ullswater
          The Rt Hon. the Lord Lovat
Social   The Marquess of Exeter
          The Earl of Lichfield
          The Viscount Ullswater
          The Lord Lovat

If a peer is a Privy Counsellor, the letters P.C. should be included after his name, office and decorations, since there is otherwise no way of knowing that he holds that office. (The usual indication for commoners who are Privy Counsellors is the inclusion of 'Rt Hon.' before their names.)

Life Peer and Life Peeress
People holding these ranks are addressed in exactly the same way as are those whose titles are hereditary.

Wife of a Peer Other Than a Duke
A Marquess's wife is a Marchioness
An Earl's wife is a Countess
A Viscount's wife is a Viscountess
A Baron's wife is a Baroness (although she is usually styled Lady...except in formal documents. A

31

Baroness in her own right, however, can exercise the female privilege of being different and call herself Baroness...).

Beginning of Letter
Formal Madam *or* Dear Madam (*not* My Lady)
Social Dear Lady Ilchester (irrespective of which of the four grades of the peerage she belongs to)

Ending of Letter
Formal Yours faithfully
Social Yours sincerely

Envelope
Formal The Most Hon. the Marchioness of Bath
The Rt Hon. the Countess of Radnor
The Rt Hon. the Viscountess Falmouth
The Rt Hon. the Lady Thurlow
Social The Marchioness of Bath
The Countess of Radnor
The Viscountess Falmouth
The Lady Thurlow

Baronet
Beginning of Letter
Formal Dear Sir *or* Sir
Social Dear Sir Richard *or*, if you don't know him well, Dear Sir Richard Williams-Bulkeley

Ending of Letter
Formal Yours faithfully
Social Yours sincerely

Envelope
Formal and Social Sir Richard Williams-Bulkeley, Bt.

Wife of Baronet
Beginning of Letter
Formal Dear Madam *or* Madam
Social Dear Lady Williams-Bulkeley

Ending of Letter
Formal Yours faithfully
Social Yours sincerely

Formal and Social Lady Williams-Bulkeley

Knight
Beginning of Letter
Formal Dear Sir *or* Sir
Social Dear Sir Jasper

Ending of Letter
Formal Yours faithfully
Social Yours sincerely

Envelope
Formal and Social Sir Jasper Brown (with the appropriate letters after his name)

Wife of Knight
This lady is addressed exactly the same as the wife of a Baronet.

Archbishops of Canterbury and York
Beginning of Letter
  Dear Archbishop

Ending of Letter
  Yours sincerely

Envelope
  The Most Reverend and Rt Hon. the Lord Archbishop of Canterbury (York)

Bishop
Beginning of Letter
  Dear Bishop

Ending of Letter
  Yours sincerely

Envelope
  The Right Reverend the Lord Bishop of Where
  or The Right Reverend the Bishop of Where

(NB The Bishop of London is always a Privy Counsellor, and envelopes to him are therefore addressed:

The Right Reverend and Rt Hon. the Lord Bishop of London)

Dean
Beginning of Letter
Dear Dean

Ending of Letter
Yours sincerely

Envelope
The Very Reverend the Dean of Lichfield

Archdeacon
Beginning of Letter
Dear Archdeacon

Ending of Letter
Yours sincerely

Envelope
The Venerable (*or* The Ven.) Archdeacon of Ely

Canon or Prebendary
Beginning of Letter
Dear Canon (*or* Prebendary)
or Dear Canon (Prebendary) Jones

Ending of Letter
Yours sincerely

Envelope
The Reverend Canon (*or* Prebendary) William Jones

Other Clergy
Beginning of Letter
Dear Mr Jackson
or Dear Father Jackson, whichever you prefer
If you are writing to the incumbent of a parish, you may use 'Dear Rector' or 'Dear Vicar' as appropriate.

Ending of Letter
  Yours sincerely

Envelope
  The Reverend John Jackson
(*Important:* Never address him either as 'Reverend Jackson' or 'The Reverend Jackson' in writing or in speech. Both are wrong...and not just because of tradition. 'Reverend' is an adjective, describing the man just as would, say, the word 'bald'. You might conceivably refer to him as 'The Bald John Jackson', but not—surely—as 'The Bald Jackson' or 'Bald Jackson'. So please save his tearing out what little hair he has left, and address the Reverend John Jackson properly, however you may find him referred to by reporters and writers who should know better. If for any reason you want to omit the word 'Reverend', 'Mr Jackson' is the expression to use.)

Privy Counsellor

Members of the Privy Council (who prefer the above spelling to the alternative *Privy Councillor*) are styled 'Right Honourable'. This expression precedes their names, and the letters P.C. follow them, after *all* decorations and honours awarded by the Crown.

There are no special forms for opening and closing letters to Privy Counsellors, whether formal or social. Use the beginning and ending appropriate to your correspondent's rank or appointment.

Envelope
Formal   The Rt Hon. the Earl of Longford, K.G., P.C.
Social   The Earl of Longford, P.C.

When addressing letters to Privy Counsellors other than peers, place 'The Rt Hon.' before the name both in formal and social usage. There is no need to include the letters P.C. afterwards. Should the person concerned be of another rank—in the Church or Armed Forces, say—then the description relevant to that rank precedes 'The Rt Hon.', thus:
  The Rt Hon. Edward Heath, M.P.

His Excellency the Rt Hon. Sir Harold Diplomat
The Rt Reverend and Rt Hon. the Lord Bishop of London
Lt. Col. the Rt Hon. Hugh There

Members of Her Majesty's Government and Opposition

Despite any inclination you may have to the contrary, you should address Members of Parliament in the same way as you would other ordinary humans, even if they have offended you.

Beginning of Letter
Formal Dear Sir *or* Dear Madam
Social Dear Mr Churchill...*or* the appropriate rank

Ending of Letter
Formal Yours faithfully
Social Yours sincerely

If you are writing to a Minister of the Crown and know him personally, you may write to him by his appointment, thus:

Dear Prime Minister
Dear Home Secretary
Dear Chancellor...and so on.

It's no longer necessary to use the cumbersome addition of Mr, Mrs or Miss before the name of the appointment, and the ending, too, is now much simpler: 'Yours sincerely' in all cases. If, however, you want to be really formal, then by all means end your letter:

I have the honour to be,
   Sir,
      Yours faithfully

But don't include the expression 'Your obedient servant'; it is obsolete. I'm sorry if that disappoints you.

Envelope
Ordinary Members of Parliament are addressed simply enough:

Mrs Jane Smith (plus any distinctions as appropriate)
    Member for Blankton
      House of Commons
        LONDON SW1A 0AA

Should, however, your correspondent also hold a ministerial or other government appointment, this too should appear in the address. So we have:

The Rt Hon. Sir Fred Barepromises, K.B.E., M.P.
    Secretary of State for Home Affairs
      House of Commons...etc.

High Court Judge

Judges of the High Court are usually knighted on appointment, or, if ladies, are created Dames. They no longer show the letters Q.C. (for Queen's Counsel) after their names.

Beginning of Letter
Formal   Dear Sir *or* Dear Madam
Social   Dear Judge *or* Dear Dame Elizabeth

Ending of Letter
Formal   Yours faithfully
Social   Yours sincerely

Envelope
Formal   *Usually* The Hon. Mr Justice Brown (without his Christian name). If, however, two judges have the same surname, the junior one always has his Christian name included in the address. And, for a Lady Judge: The Hon. Mrs Justice Lane
Social   Sir John Brown *or* Dame Elizabeth Lane

Circuit Judge

Beginning of Letter
Formal   Dear Sir *or* Dear Madam
Social   Dear Judge

Ending of Letter
Formal   Yours faithfully
Social   Yours sincerely

Envelope

All occasions   His (or Her) Honour Judge Brown
Here again, don't include the Christian name unless you know another circuit judge with a similar surname is at the same address.

If you know the judge to be a Knight, you should address the envelope as follows:

Formal   His Honour Judge Sir John Brown
Social   Sir John Brown

Untitled Gentleman

The choice between Mr and Esq. is yours; either is regarded as correct in the United Kingdom and Ireland, although Australia, Canada, New Zealand, and the United States of America generally prefer Mr. Never play safe and use both: Mr Charles Smith is fine, and so is Charles Smith, Esq. Mr Charles Smith, Esq. is wrong at both ends.

The use of the plain name, e.g. Charles Smith, is considered impolite, except for schoolboys. These young gentlemen nowadays dislike being addressed as 'Master', and that term has largely gone out of fashion, although it can be used for small boys up to the age of about eight years. Even they, however, usually prefer to be rid of the mark of the beast as soon as possible, so if you want to be certain not to incur their wrath, it is no doubt best to stay with the plain name until they deserve better.

Untitled Married Lady

We have seen in the last chapter that this lady is almost invariably addressed as Mrs. While the opening of the letter—Dear Mrs Jones—is straightforward enough, there are certain rules covering the correct way of expressing her name or initials on the envelope; these are best explained by means of examples.

Envelope
(a) Wife or widow of the head of the family,

provided no senior widow is still living:
Mrs Jones (no Christian name or initials)
(b) Wives or widows of other members of the family:
Mrs David Jones *or* Mrs D. A. Jones
(her husband's name or initials)
(NB A mistake often made is to address a widow by her own name or initials. This is incorrect, since it implies that her husband has departed other than by dying; the form is reserved for divorced ladies.)
(c) Divorced ladies:
Mrs Josephine Jones *or*, more usually preferred, Mrs J. Jones (her own initials)

Clearly, however, there will be times when the above rules must be interpreted more liberally and in accordance with the circumstances. If you are, for instance, writing a business letter to a married woman, it is unlikely that you would know her husband's name or initials, and the sensible thing to do then is to use her own.

Untitled Unmarried Lady
Whether a lady is married or single, formal letters to her begin 'Dear Madam', while social ones start 'Dear Miss Rix'. The correct endings are, respectively, 'Yours faithfully' and 'Yours sincerely'. Addressing the envelope introduces an element of choice, depending on what seniority she occupies in the household.

Envelope
(a) Eldest unmarried daughter of the senior generation:
Miss Rix
otherwise
Miss Arabella Rix

Lady of Undisclosed Marital Status
In Chapter Five I mention the modern use of Ms by ladies who prefer not to disclose their marital status. They are usually, but not always, members of the professions or engaged in business. While the practice

is logical and becoming more generally accepted, it should be mentioned that it still offends many more than it pleases, so it is prudent not to use it unless the lady has indicated that she prefers you to do so.

Correspondence with Firms

It is usually best to address such correspondence to the person for whom it is intended, preferably by his appointment or, by his name (if you know it) and appointment. This will ensure that it reaches the right destination as quickly as possible.

Remember, however, the caution I gave earlier about the use of an individual's name: should he be away, it is possible that your letter might wait a long time before he sees it; and the longer it lies around his office, the more chance it has of going astray. Mail addressed to The Managing Director, The Company Secretary, the Chairman, The Sales Director, and the like will be certain to be opened in the right department and attended to quickly. Should the person you're writing to be away, your letter will then be dealt with as required by someone deputizing for him.

'Dear Sir' or 'Dear Sirs' is always a correct way of beginning business correspondence, although if you know the person to whom you are writing is a lady then you would do better to use 'Dear Madam' or to address her by name in the letter. And 'Yours faithfully' or 'Yours truly' as appropriate is the right way to end. When one firm is writing to another, firm to firm, as it were, 'Gentlemen' is sometimes used instead of 'Dear Sirs', and the same opening can be used by an individual writing to a large group or organization. My own preference, however, is to stay with 'Dear Sirs' in such circumstances: there seems little point in introducing needless complications.

At the risk of offending some of my readers, I have to say that the term 'Mesdames' as the feminine equivalent of 'Sirs' is rarely used in business circles, either in the body of the letter or on the envelope. If you are concerned to be as accurate as possible and know that you are writing to a lady, you can avoid the problem by addressing her in person: 'Ms A. Black, Managing Director'; and, at the start of the letter: 'Dear Ms Black'.

Messrs: When to Use It and When Not To   This term, a contraction of the French word *Messieurs*, is used in English as the plural of 'Mr'. It is not normally adopted in Canada or the United States of America, and is falling from general use in Australia, Britain, and New Zealand. Certain professions, notably the law, do, however, still employ it, so you would be correct in addressing a letter to a firm of solicitors as, say, Messrs Leach and Raptor if such was its name.

If, in spite of the above, you still feel a letter to a firm isn't quite right without the 'Messrs', restrict its use to those businesses with personal names. Thus:

Messrs Dolittle and Seldom
Messrs Caliban and Mordred Spong
Messrs Adam Bachelor and Sons

You should *never* use 'Messrs' in the following cases:
1 Firms with a lady's name, e.g. Jane Brown and Co.
2 Firms whose name includes a title,
   e.g. Sir Archibald Molestrangler and Associates
3 Firms not trading under a surname, or in which the surname does not form the complete business name, e.g.:
   Anglesey and Wapping World Airlines
   The Knightsbridge Rubber Humbug Company
   Julian Smallpeace's School of Unarmed Combat
   The Letitia Swepoff Theatrical Agency
4 Limited Companies, whether private (Ltd) or public (PLC). This might surprise some readers, but the reason is a simple one: in law a limited company is considered a single entity (that is, as an individual), and 'Messrs' refers to more than one individual.

This chapter has covered most of the titles and forms of address likely to be encountered in ordinary correspondence. The subject, however, is a complicated one if you wish to observe the fine detail of protocol, and lack of space prevents the inclusion here of the less frequently used forms and of the customs of many overseas countries. The styles used to address members of Her Majesty's Armed Forces, for example, especially those of commissioned rank, are perhaps of immediate interest to a comparatively small proportion of readers and have therefore been omitted.

For readers needing to know more, there are available both in libraries and bookshops several books dealing with the topic in depth. Of these an excellent choice would be *Debrett's Correct Form*, widely recognized as authoritative and which has served me well in my own work over the years.

Chapter Five
ABBREVIATIONS

As a general rule, *initials* used as a form of abbreviation are followed by a full stop, known also as a full point. So if you receive a cheque from your bank manager bearing the initials R.D., you will know he is anxious that you should regard his note as something more than a shortened form of 'road'. Where, however, the abbreviation consists only of *capital letters* or forms a *recognized acronym*, often pronounced as a single word, there is no need to use full stops. Examples are: BBC, HMS, PAYE, RSVP, Anzac, Fiat, SOGAT. Initials of personal names usually require a full stop, although the house styles of certain companies occasionally dispense with it.

If the abbreviation or contraction consists of a *mixture of capital letters and small ones*, it usually takes full points as in, say, I.o.M. (Isle of Man), Bt. (Baronet), or Kt. (Knight). But there is an increasing tendency nowadays to dispense with the stop if the first and last letters of the shortened form are the same as those of the complete one. So you have Ltd, Mr, Mrs, Mme, Mlle, Dr, and Revd—although if you omit that last 'd' when writing to your local clergyman, you must replace it with a full stop.

Modern usage has given us a convenient term for use when you're not sure whether the lady to whom you are writing is married or single, or if she prefers not to distinguish between the two states. 'Ms'—pronounced 'miz'—is not, strictly speaking, an abbreviation at all and as such does not take a full stop. Don't however, write it 'MS' which is the standard short form of 'manuscript'.

Similarly, modern practice allows Ave, Rd, and St as accepted shortened versions of 'Avenue', 'Road', and 'Street'.

It is best to avoid shortening the names of *days* and *months* whenever possible, but if you really must abbreviate them, the following are recognized:

Sun. Mon. Tue. Wed. Thur. Fri. Sat.

Jan. Feb. Mar. Apr. May June

July Aug. Sept. Oct. Nov. Dec.

County names, when shortened, take a full stop at the end...with two exceptions: Hampshire, whose abbreviation 'Hants' is very old and is traditionally written without the concluding dot; and Shropshire, where the old name 'Salop' similarly remains unpunctuated. Be careful, however, with some of the newer counties in the United Kingdom: many of them have names which are already short and neither require abbreviation nor would lend themselves readily to it anyway. Thus, for example, Avon and Gwynedd remain uncut and undotted.

Difficulty is occasionally encountered in shortening some words used in everyday *measurements*, especially in their plural forms. You will avoid this if you remember the simple rule that the abbreviations for both singular and plural terms are almost always the same. Thus we have: in., ft., oz., lb., cwt., mm., cm., kg., sec., and min. While most authorities adopt the style I have shown, it is to some extent a matter of taste whether you use the full stop when the first and last letters of the above abbreviations are the same as those of the full word. Either custom is accepted as correct.

The increasing pace of modern living seems to require that more and more words and expressions be referred to by their initials or some other shortened form. The number of abbreviations in common use is being added to constantly, and their scope is so wide that it is impractical to attempt to list them here.

Chapter Six
BUSINESS LETTERS

Business has constructed a language of its own. The businessman tells us that door handles are *in short supply,* that he has *updated* his latest order of them, and that at the next meeting of the board he will *finalize* his arrangements for *shipping* them. What he means is that door handles are scarce, that he has ordered some more, and that at the next board meeting he will complete arrangements for sending them.

Each of us, every day, speaks a language that is familiar to us and relevant to our lives. Our businessman above is doing just that. His impressive words invest with adventure the ordinary events of his everyday life; he gallops among his door handles arrayed as a knight. And we should be tolerant of his fancies, for what man of spirit doesn't secretly long to ride a white horse, if only figuratively? But we have to ask ourselves whether his special language is helpful either to him or to the people to whom it is addressed. With a little effort, the same ideas can be expressed more clearly and much more forcibly by the use of less daunting and simpler language. Too often, the special words of business seem better aimed at voicing the user's dreams than at expressing his precise meaning.

The whole idea of writing any letter, but especially one on business, is to convey information and usually to evoke some action. To do this we must observe two simple rules: we must write in language that is easily understood; and we mustn't bore the reader. The second requirement is tied closely to the first.

Short words almost always work better than long ones. Equally important, they leave little room for misunderstanding, so they are more likely to produce the results we want. We can't avoid employing some long words, of course, but we should choose and use them carefully. Too often they're included for no other reason than that we think they impress, when in reality they cloud the issue and make our letter look less urgent. Let's look at two possible letters from your bank manager. The first goes something like this:

> Your recent drawings have been increasingly and steadily exceeding the mutually-agreed credit limit, and I feel it incumbent on me to insist on your promptly depositing funds sufficient to bring your account balance to an acceptable level.

The second says:

> Your overdraft is well past the limit and getting bigger. Please pay in at once enough funds to bring it down to the figure we agreed.

Which of those two letters is more likely to give you the impression that the gentleman is trying to tell you something and wants you to take some urgent action? If you want your letters to seem important, keep them short and to the point. And use words that are easy to understand. You can do it without being impolite, and you won't run the risk of boring your correspondent.

When we bore our reader, all communication between us and them breaks down, and from that point on we are wasting our time. We might also be wasting theirs, but the chances of that are less because they will probably have ceased to pay attention to what has been written. A letter can look boring even before you begin to read it, and it is a good idea to check any letter you have written, before you seal the envelope, just to see what it looks like. Just as a person's voice can be boring or interesting, so can his letters; short sentences and familiar words have life and energy and are much easier to understand than a long-winded style, full of needlessly complicated language.

The certain way to avoid boring the other person is to keep within the limits of his interest. If you want to say something that might not immediately interest him, you have to find a way to extend his attention. And the best method of doing this is to make sure that he is involved in what you're saying. Remember what the redhead said when her new boyfriend tried to find out what best amused her: 'Let's talk about me'. 'Me' is everyone's favourite subject, however we might try to deny it, and the wise writer does well to remember it. So try to relate what you're writing to the other person and his interests.

The old business cliché about time being money is generally true. Most folk involved in business consider themselves short of time, and with the growth of communications there is almost always too much to read: memos and letters crowd the in-trays, this month's trade magazines arrive before last month's have been opened, and there is a never-ending stream of miscellaneous documents demanding attention. So the surest way to bore your correspondent instantly and to make him take less notice of your letter than you want is to write too much. The length of what you write must relate directly to what interests *him;* as soon as you've reached that limit, stop.

The other chap might have a lot on his plate when your letter reaches him. The easiest way for you to interest him and to keep his interest is to make things easy for him; he'll then be half way towards seeing your point of view. Most of us, when we write something, use words

which we rarely, if ever, use in everyday speech. Before sending your letter, re-read it, and if it sounds heavy-going, look at all those words which you wouldn't normally use in conversation. Ask yourself honestly whether your letter would be any the worse without them, and if they're not essential change them to words you would speak.

So remember:

1 Keep it within the limits of your reader's interests.
2 Keep it short and to the point.
3 Keep it simple and straightforward.

The process of writing a business letter is much the same as writing any other, except that one needs to take special care to make it well directed. Unlike personal correspondence, where what might be described as background information—snippets of personal news, asides, general gossip, and the like—is not only permissible but often desirable, the business letter should come straight to the point, make it clearly and politely, and then just as politely close.

Be careful to observe the ordinary courtesies of a letter: your address, your correspondent's address, and the date. The ways of setting these out are covered in full earlier in this book, and by now you will be familiar with them, but let me make one important point about the date. Often, in business transactions at all levels, the date has especial relevance: it might be the deciding factor as to whether an order is filled, an account is paid, or a guarantee claim is met. On many occasions, its effects could be even more far-reaching. All of our lives are ruled to some degree by the clock and the calendar, and nowhere more so than in

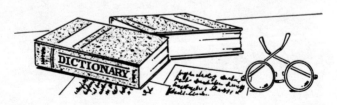

business, so it makes sense to ensure that your letter bears the correct date.

Never adopt the sloppy and discourteous practice of inserting the standard phrase 'Date as postmark' at the top of your correspondence. Nothing is more certain to convince the recipient that you couldn't care less about him personally than this evidence that the letter is one of a broadside being sent out to all and sundry. My personal reaction is never to attach any importance to a letter so dated. On a more practical level, however, it is worth remembering that postmarks are often indistinct, and that in many firms the post is opened at a central point, the envelopes discarded, and the letters distributed to the people concerned. So much then for the 'Date as postmark'.

Before we leave the subject of the date, do make sure that you post the letter promptly. By all means promise to sue that tight-fisted so-and-so if he doesn't pay up within a week. But don't cut the ground from beneath your feet by letting the postmark reveal that you couldn't be bothered to mail the letter for five days after you wrote it. Apart from the effect it will have on your creditor, it won't help your case if you do have to take the matter to court.

You will often receive letters requiring you to reply, and in most cases these will bear the sender's *reference*. This can take several forms. Should your local tax office feel constrained to write to you, it might be your file number. If the letter comes from a department within a large organization the reference could be no more than a simple note of the sender's and typist's initials. Or it might look like the logarithm of the national debt. This latter will almost always emanate from one of three sources: a local authority or a service industry; or a mail-order firm informing you that you have been personally selected to be one of millions in a prize draw if you buy a collection of records of the mating calls of British freshwater fish.

Whatever the reference, however, it will generally help

speed matters along if you quote it at the head of your letter, at the left-hand side and opposite the date. In the event of its being of the logarithm variety, you could well find that it fits more easily on a line by itself, neatly underlined, between the 'Dear Sir' opening and the first line of the body of the letter. An example of this is given on page 52.

You might find it useful to have your own reference, especially if you are sending out letters to a number of correspondents and all dealing with the same subject. In this case, place the reference, as before, opposite the date, but on the line beneath the recipient's, should there be one. Indicate clearly which is which, thus:

Your reference: ABC/de
My (*or* Our) Reference: 12345/XYZ

At the beginning of the chapter I observed that business has constructed a language of its own. In saying that I didn't mean the use of terms peculiar to technology, science, and industry. I meant the stilted, convoluted, and meaningless phrases which some folk feel are demanded of them once they sit down to compose anything coming under the general heading of business. Let's look at the sort of thing you *shouldn't* write.

Your Reference: MR/big
Our Reference: AC/nbg   2 July 19—

Messrs Acme Spridgets Limited
101 High Street
ANYTOWN
Staffs.
AN9 6LL

Dear Sirs,
    We are in receipt of your esteemed favour and order of the 28th ult. and beg to confirm that we shall spare no effort to expedite despatch in accordance with your expressed instructions. We currently have an in-stock situation of grommet tremblers and anticipate shipment without delay so that you might expect them at your earliest convenience.

Assuring you of our best attention at all times,
Yours respectfully,
p.p. Messrs Universal Grommet Tremblers Limited

A. Creep
Sales Director

The effect of the above is much like that of rounding
Cape Horn in a rubber dinghy after a satisfying meal of
fat pork. There are thousands of letters just like that
whizzing around at this very moment. In the interests
of good digestion, therefore, let's see the sort of thing
that I'm sure you send out every day.

Your Reference: MR/big
Our Reference: IAMW/VG   2 July 19—

The Buying Manager
Acme Spridgets Limited
101 High Street
ANYTOWN
Staffs.
AN9 6LL

Dear Mr Buggins, [or Dear Sir if you don't know him]
    Thank you for your order of 28 June 19— for 500
grommet tremblers. We have them in stock and are sending
them at once, so you can expect them by the carrier's first
delivery.
Yours sincerely, [or faithfully]
p.p. Universal Grommet Tremblers Limited

I. A. M. Wright
Sales Director

Apart from the more obvious improvements shown by
the second letter, you may have noticed two points
needing explanation. The first letter contained, buried
among the general ooze, a reference to '28th ult'; and
both letters included the abbreviation 'p.p.'. What do
they mean, and why is one acceptable and the other
not?

'Ult.' is one of a series—ult., inst., and prox.—which are
shortened forms of *'ultimo mense', 'instant',* and
'proximo mense'. Unless you are writing to a Roman
legionnaire or anyone else for whom Latin is the
everyday tongue, you'd be better off using the English

equivalents: last month, this month, and next month. And, if you want to make things really easy, why not do as Mr Wright did in the second letter above... and just use the name of the month?

The second of those abbreviations, 'p.p.', while still representing a Latin phrase *(per procurationem),* is more sensible and acceptable. The expression is also sometimes written as 'per pro', but the meaning is still the same: 'by proxy', or 'for and on behalf of'; while the latter phrase is occasionally used, 'p.p.' has become generally accepted and understood... and it's shorter. A word of caution here, however: notice that the 'p.p.' goes in front of the firm or person on whose behalf the letter is being signed, not the name of the person signing. Secretaries and personal assistants please note.

Now for an example showing the way in which you can easily quote a reference which might otherwise be unwieldy.

14 December 19—

Booklovers Heritage Mint Limited
15b Punters Court
LONDON
EC1X 9YZ

Dear Sirs,
  Ref: 000123678EGKD14—3467/00001000853 99.5
  Book of Manx Toads and Snakes
  Thank you for my free polythene eggcup and my six entry certificates for your annual draw. I see from the secret code revealed by the coloured spectacles you supplied that I qualify for an extra four million pounds because I sent in my order promptly.
  I shall look forward to banking my extra winnings and to driving the tractor awarded as first prize, but it seems you know more about our village than I do. The nearest thing we have to a bank is the coin box in the local telephone kiosk. Please where *is* the Dumbleton branch of the National Midclays Bank?
Yours faithfully,

I. Vadenough

Chapter Seven
PERSONAL LETTERS

Before the advent of newer methods of communication and of faster and more reliable means of transport, the letter was often the only way in which families and friends could keep in touch. Nowadays, the more widespread use of the telephone, and the ability to fly from one side of the world to the other in a matter of hours have made it easier to speak to absent friends in person. And if we're honest with ourselves, we must, I suspect, admit that natural laziness seizes its opportunity whenever it can; it is quicker, and takes less effort, to pick up a telephone and dial a number than to sit down and compose a carefully thought out letter.

Yet it is worth remembering that, for all its advantages, a telephone call is an impermanent thing. Save in the rare cases where the recipient is able and takes the trouble to record it, once ended it has gone for ever. It cannot be brought out time and time again to delight the heart, to awaken fond memories, or just to confirm forgotten facts. A letter can; and down the years it often assumes a depth of meaning and value undreamed of by its writer or even by the receiver.

PERSONAL LETTERS

Many people find that the personal letter is more difficult to write than that on business. There the subject matter more often than not chooses itself; after all, you don't decide to write a business letter for fun. And in most cases we have a clear idea of what needs to be said and how to say it.

Often, however, the task of penning a personal letter assumes almost overwhelming proportions: we know we *ought* to write, we *want* to write, but we can think of little to say. Or, if we can, we don't know how to say it. Perhaps we might create the wrong impression. What if we give offence? What use can a letter be to someone who has lost a loved one, save only to reopen the wound? It is doubts like these that so often prevent us from writing the letter which might make all the difference to the other person. But we must write, so how do we set about it?

First of all, make a start. Thinking about something is the most frequent excuse for not doing it; and, if it's any consolation, most professional writers (the honest ones, that is) use it almost every day. It's probably true to say that if you put off writing a personal letter long enough the need for it will disappear anyway, but it leaves a nasty feeling that we have let someone down. And we usually have. So sit down, open your pad, uncap your pen, and begin writing.

At first it doesn't matter what you write; the important thing is that you've started. You'll find it easy enough to scrap what you've written and begin anew if you're not happy with your first effort. And the feeling of self-righteousness you get when you've finished a letter that you've been putting off for days is marvellous.

I'm often asked for advice on how long a personal letter should be. That merits the same answer as 'How long is a piece of string?' It all depends on what you want it to do. So the examples which follow should be regarded as guides rather than models which can be slavishly copied. You'll sometimes find that, once you have begun to write, an almost endless stream of things you want to say comes into your head; if that's so, then by all means carry on until you've said them all. Occasionally, depending on the reason which prompts your letter, you will know that you and your correspondent will be best served by fewer words. Again, don't think there is any rule compelling you to waffle on; there isn't. Nor is there any need for you to write perfectly grammatical English; indeed, when it is appropriate, the chatty letter, worded in the same way as you would speak, is of greater effect and means much more to the other person.

Clearly, no book can provide examples of all the many types of personal letter you can send. I offer the following in the hope that they will be helpful on some of those occasions when perhaps a little extra care is required—say, for reasons of tact, or because the situation is one where you need a signpost showing a safe way to go.

Some letters are more difficult to write than others, so we'll look first at a few of the easier ones, and then tackle those needing, perhaps, a more sensitive approach.

The Thank-you Letter

This isn't always as easy to write as may at first appear. Not all gifts are welcome. Some are an embarrassment (as any newly-married couple with half a dozen electric toasters, all simultaneously displayed, will confirm); some are disappointing, like the pair of socks you get when you've been expecting a wrist watch; and some can be just plain unwanted—as when Great Aunt Jane gives you the set of three flying china ducks that you've always wished would fall off her wall.

It's as well to remember, however, that gifts, in whatever form, are generally made with the best of intentions, so take care to word your letter so as not to hurt or give offence to the person you're writing to. 'Thanks for the tie. It brings my collection of blue ones up to the 500 mark' is not quite the way to go about it. The following might help.

55

Wedding Gift

Thank you so much for the electric toaster you sent us as a wedding present; you must have given a lot of thought to it, because it's the sort of thing any young couple would find very useful. And you were the only one to think of so practical a gift. [*N.B.* The last sentence can easily be left out if your kitchen closely resembles a toaster stockroom... but remember to make sure that only the right one is on display when the donor pays a visit. This can become complicated without some form of list and cross-referencing, and is doubtless one of the reasons behind the home computer boom.]

Tom and I have never been particularly early risers, and now that there are two of us to get off to work you can be sure that your gift will be put to good use in saving those extra few minutes each morning. What's more we won't run the risk of burning the house down by forgetting toast under the grill.

We have only just returned from honeymoon (a wonderful time—I'll tell you about it later), and there are so many things to do in getting the house ready. Will you forgive this short note, then? I promise I'll write more during the next couple of weeks, but I did so want to tell you how much we appreciate your kindness, and both of us send you our love and best wishes.

Birthday and Christmas Gifts

What a lovely surprise! When I opened the parcel and saw the blue tie packed so neatly inside, I knew it could have come only from you. It is beautifully made and exactly the sort of thing I wear. You must have known that blue is my favourite colour. Thank you so much for your kind thought; it's nice to know you think of me at these times.

(*NB* You will see that the above would be equally suitable, whether this was your 500th blue tie or the one you'd had your heart set on for months. It's truthful, and it doesn't make you sound ungrateful.)

It is usual and courteous to expand this sort of letter into a more newsy one, and the degree to which you do this will depend on circumstances. A letter to a relative or close friend will naturally warrant more than would one, say, to a business associate whom you didn't know especially closely.

The essential thing is to make the other person feel that he really chose exactly the right gift for you and that, irrespective of how many you have received (and don't tell him how many), his is the only one that really pleased you. Put yourself in his place and write as you would hope to be written to.

For Services Rendered

John and I arrived back from holiday yesterday after a wonderful time in the Isle of Man, but dreading the job of getting the garden back into shape again after four weeks away. Imagine our delight, then, to find the lawns neatly mown and all the borders tidy. Even the vegetable plot was free of weeds. Old Mrs Jones next door popped in just after we got back to tell us that a young couple in a red Volkswagen had been round every weekend to keep an eye on things, as she put it.

Even had you not been the only folk we know with a red Volkswagen, we would have known at once who were the good Samaritans. Thank you so much. You'll never know just how much your kindness means to us; it put the perfect seal on a perfect holiday.

It's also put us in something of a spot. We had in any case brought you a small gift back from Douglas, but now it might seem like an afterthought. You won't think that, will you? If you had seen John's face when he realised that he hadn't got to spend all that time tidying up, you would know that nothing we could have brought you would have even begun to repay your thoughtfulness.

We were going to call to see you next Thursday, but we would be so pleased if you could manage to come over and spend the day with us on Sunday. As John says, if the weather is fine we can eat out of doors... the garden is looking lovely. I'll ring you tomorrow evening to confirm times, but I just had to write at once to say how much we appreciate your kindness. (I've not even begun to unpack yet).

After a Visit or a Party

Increasingly, the telephone is being used as a means of conveying thanks after visits or parties, and sometimes even after the receipt of a gift. If, however, someone has clearly gone to considerable trouble on your behalf or has given a gift where none was expected—perhaps not even deserved—a letter is really called for. The extra effort and thought required is always appreciated.

> It was kind of you to ask Mary and me to spend the weekend with you. Her recent illness had left its mark, as you know, and this break was just what she needed to restore her to her old self. She says she feels like a new woman... and I resisted the temptation to say that I'd often felt like one myself; I'm too young to die.
>
> To be serious, though, we both enjoyed ourselves more than we can say, and your kindness in arranging theatre seats for the four of us on Saturday was an added delight. We can't remember when we last had so much fun. Thank you so much for all the trouble you took; it meant such a lot to us.
>
> When we arrived home, we found that the children...

* * * *

We turn now to a few occasions when a little more forethought is required before we write our letter. Congratulations, for example, can so often sound trite and insincere, even when genuinely meant. And a letter of condolence, perhaps one of the most difficult to write well, is rarely tackled with confidence, usually from a sense of inadequacy at a time of great personal sadness.

Invitations

Most formal invitations, such as those to weddings or official functions, are sent out in the form of specially printed cards; a selection of suitable wording is always shown in the printer's catalogue from which the stationer will help you make your choice. If you prefer the personal touch of sending out your own, it is still best—especially if large numbers are involved—to use a formal layout along the following lines.

Wedding

> Mr and Mrs Archibald Custerd
> request the pleasure of the company of
>
> ....Mr.and.Mrs.R..U..Barben............................
>
> at the marriage of their daughter
> *Prunella*
> with
> *Mr Stewart Thomas Baggs*
> at St Trinian's Parish Church, Wrexham
> on Saturday, 23 June 19--, at 11.00 a.m.
> and afterwards at The Pen y Sillyn Arms, Mold
>
> 22 Movington Close   R.S.V.P.
> Hopeton

R.S.V.P. is not, of course, an indication of what is to be served at the reception. An abbreviation of the French *Répondez s'il vous plaît'*, it translates as 'Please reply'.

General Invitation — Formal

> Mr and Mrs Robert Topers request the pleasure of
> Miss Alice Tippler's company on
> Friday 18 September, 19--, at 7.00p.m.
>
> COCKTAILS
>
> 3 Elbows Bend   R.S.V.P.
>
> Beer, Devon

Informal Invitations

Despite the increasing use of the telephone, many people still prefer to send out informal invitations by letter. Apart from making the event appear just that little more well-planned and important, the practice has the advantage of putting the details of the event—its date, time, and place—on more permanent record. And, as anyone who has forgotten the address of a reception will know, that can save a lot of headaches all round.

> Jim and I are having a few friends round to the house for bridge on Tuesday evening next (5 December), and we would be delighted if you could come. We plan to start at 8.00 o'clock. Please don't go to the trouble of evening dress, as everything will be informal.

Notice that, although this letter is little more than a chatty note, all the relevant details are given. The address and telephone number will, of course, be at the head of the notepaper as usual, and the body of the letter gives the day, date, time, and information as to what sort of dress the guest is to wear.

Acceptances and Refusals

Acceptances generally pose fewer problems than refusals; after all, you don't have to think how to say 'no' without hurting someone's feelings. Although it is possible to buy preprinted acceptance cards for formal invitations, it really isn't worth it: they have so many spaces to be filled in that you might as well write the whole thing yourself. Using good-quality notepaper—as always—and making sure that it shows the address, telephone number, and the date, let's accept or politely decline the invitations given above.

Wedding

> Mr and Mrs Ronald Barben thank Mr and Mrs Archibald Custerd for their kind invitation to the marriage of their daughter Prunella at St Trinian's Parish Church on Saturday, 23 June, and have great pleasure in accepting [or] and much regret that they will be unable to attend as they will be out of the country on that date.

A formal invitation does not necessarily demand a formal reply. It is perfectly acceptable, especially where the people involved are all friends, for the reply to take the form of a simple, informal letter. Indeed, if you have to decline the invitation, it is usually easier and kinder to do this tactfully in a short letter of explanation.

Thank you so much for your kind invitation to Prunella's wedding on 23 June. Ronald and I would love to be there on her great day, but I'm sorry to say that it coincides with the time when we shall be away on holiday. Please give her and Stewart our love and best wishes and tell them that we shall be thinking of them. We have sent them a small gift which we hope will be useful to them in their new home, so tell Prunella to keep an eye open for the parcels delivery during the next few days.

General

Miss Alice Tippler has much pleasure in accepting Mr and Mrs Topers' invitation kind invitation to cocktails on Friday, 18 September, at 7.00 p.m.

Note how, in this formal acceptance, Alice has repeated the relevant details of the engagement. It is not unknown for the occasional error to creep into an invitation, and her arrival at, for example, 5.00 p.m. would probably be both inconvenient and embarrassing. She might, however, have replied less formally, perhaps like this:

Thank you both very much for your kind invitation to cocktails next Friday evening (the 18th) at 7 o'clock. I should love to come, and am looking forward to seeing you both again after such a long time.

If she is unable to accept, she might write:

...love to come, but I already have a long-standing engagement on that evening, and I know you will understand that it would be impolite to cancel it. I'm so disappointed, for we haven't met for such a long time and I would have loved to see you again. I'll ring you early next week for a chat, and we'll see if we can arrange something soon.

And, for the bridge invitation, a friendly reply might run:

It was kind of you and Jim to think of me when arranging your bridge evening. Thank you very much. I'd be so pleased to come along, and I shall look forward to being with you both again next Tuesday (the 5th) evening at 8 o'clock.

Similarly, a refusal can be made equally friendly.

> ... Thank you very much. I'm really very sorry, but I won't be able to make it this time: my final examinations take place that evening, and you'll understand that I must put in an appearance. There are no prizes, however, for guessing where I'd rather be on that day. I'd been looking forward to our next bridge party together.

It is always best to decline an invitation politely and to try to convey a sense of real regret, even if you don't really want to attend the function. Most invitations arrive because the senders genuinely want you to be there. Even if they don't and are acting from nothing more than a sense of courtesy, they've still taken the trouble to invite you. Good manners require you at least not to hurt their feelings, and on a more selfish if still practical level, life is too short for us to offend people, even those we don't like.

Congratulations

There should be no more difficulty in writing a letter of congratulations than in penning any other sort, although some people tend to fight shy of it. Adopt the same approach as in any form of writing: be sincere and sound sincere. If you are genuinely pleased with the other person's success, then don't be afraid to let your feelings show in your writing. In fact, the more they show the better your letter will be. If you are writing out of nothing more than politeness, don't, for goodness' sake, affect an enthusiasm that isn't there; it will show. Just say what you have to say, politely and tactfully, and leave it at that.

> What wonderful news! I've been practising for ages what I would say to you both when you finally managed your joint production, but now that it's happened I'm lost for words. I'm so pleased for you both, and especially that the baby is a boy, for I know how much you both wanted one.
>
> Since you, Jane, appear to have had the harder task these last few days, I suppose the greater part of my congratulations should go to you. But, knowing what Dad has to go through in the coming years, I think I'd better

share them equally with Tom. Well done, both of you. I'm delighted to know that Jane and the baby are doing well and that Tom, too, is bearing up under the strain. I will be round to see the whole family in a week or two, when you have had a chance to settle down, and I'm looking forward to meeting the smallest Smith.

More formally, and perhaps more from a sense of duty than desire:

I must write to congratulate you on your election as mayor for the coming year. It is a great honour, and one towards which you have clearly been working hard for a long time. No-one deserves it more than you, and I am sure that you will bring to this high office the same degree of dedication and competence which is so evident in all your public work.

Read the above letter carefully. It can not possibly offend and will almost certainly please the recipient. But, depending on your personal opinion of local politics and this person in particular, it can cover a multitude of sins equally appropriately. Either way you are being sincere without running the risk of displeasing.

Condolences and Sympathy

If there is one branch of letter writing which can be said to cause problems, this is probably it. Not that it requires any more skill with words than any other; it doesn't. But when it falls to us to express sympathy, especially in a bereavement, we usually feel so inadequate that we think any words we might say will be useless anyway. This is a natural reaction, but we should remember that here is an opportunity to do a little good, and the effort is well worth while and always appreciated.

Some people have a natural aptitude for this sort of letter. They will not need any advice, for at such times the heart takes over the pen. If you are one of the many who find real difficulty, it is best to keep your letter short and simple. Remember that to a bereaved person an arm round the shoulder means at least as much as, if not more than, effusive expressions of sympathy. Make your letter figuratively that arm round the shoulder.

> Mary and I were greatly shocked and saddened to hear of Jim's sudden death yesterday. I know that at such times words seem empty and useless. But we want you to know that we understand, my dear, and that if we can be of any help to you—in any way—you have only to tell us.

It is unnecessary, and generally inappropriate, to refer to the many significant things the deceased has done in his life. There is a place for such details, of course, and this is usually in a newspaper obituary or similar public tribute. But your writing is intended to show the bereaved person that you are sincerely sad to hear of their loss, to offer your condolences, and similarly to offer any help you might feel able to give. It is important not to fill your letter with weeping and wailing; the occasion is sad enough as it is, and your aim is to comfort rather than to hurt an open wound by well-intentioned but ill-advised words.

Other occasions may prompt us to send letters of sympathy. A fire, perhaps, or an accident. Or maybe a divorce. It is difficult to give very specific guidance for such times, but the one sound basic rule which will guide you always is that we have referred to many times already: put yourself in the other person's place, and don't write anything that will hurt or embarrass them.

Divorce is an especially painful time for all concerned, no matter how brave or cavalier a face they may put on it. A well-meant letter from you offering comfort and help and, for good measure, implying that she's well rid of the brute, might cause untold harm. The following example should help you tread safely the delicate and dangerous path through the mental jungle of the recently divorced person.

> Richard and I were very sorry to hear of your divorce last week, and wonder if there is anything we can do to help. We had been such good friends with yourself and Alan, and it is always sad to see a marriage break up, whatever the reason.

Although we can only begin to guess at the pain and stress the whole business must have caused you, we want you to know that you can call on us if you feel in need of practical help or even just a talk. You have often told us we were your best friends, so now we'd like to do something to justify the description.

I will give you a ring in a couple of days and we can have a chat. Who knows, we might even get round to arranging a trip into town for that meal we've been promising ourselves for the last few months... just us two girls.

You will see how, in the above, I have carefully avoided siding with either party, whoever might have been to blame, if blame there were. And, in suggesting a meal together for the two girls, I've given the newly-divorced woman a chance to take up the old family friendship again, this time on her own behalf. To sidestep the inevitable embarrassment of her being the odd one of three (a problem facing all divorced persons at one time or another, and a particularly painful one in the early days), I have suggested a meal for just the two ladies.

Answering Letters

It might at first seem that a letter written in answer to one already received is by far the easiest to write and that there's not much advice anyone can give on the subject. I would agree with the first part of that assumption, but wouldn't be so ready to do so with the second.

You see, there are two things you can do when answering a letter, and as often as not people omit half the first and forget about the second when it is applicable. So what are these important points?

The first, and most obvious, is that you should answer the letter. I correspond regularly with a cousin who lives in Australia and have been trying without success to get a reply to a question I first asked in a letter more than a year ago. It's not that he won't answer it (at least, I can think of no reason why he wouldn't want to do so), but simply that he often takes his time before replying and then has so much to say that he forgets what we were discussing in earlier letters.

This sort of thing can be very annoying to your correspondent, and it is easy enough to avoid doing it. First, answer the letter as soon as possible. We all know that the longer a letter sits on the shelf awaiting an answer the less we feel like writing (because of reluctance to acknowledge the delay, if we're honest), and so the less likely we are to answer it. Moreover, much of the news it contains might well be out of date by the time we get round to it.

Next, have the original letter by you when you are answering it. Go through it as you write, and tick off the points requiring attention as you deal with them. You'll be pleasantly surprised at how easy it is to write quite a long letter, merely by replying to questions and news passed on by your correspondent when last he wrote.

You'll also find your replies generating new ideas and thoughts which you'll want to add, and so the problem of what to write disappears. And this is the second thing you can do when answering a letter. A helpful practice in personal correspondence, it can be turned to practical advantage in business letters when, for example, an enquiry from a potential customer about one product can be used as a means of introducing others. So don't put off answering letters, will you? It's much easier to do it at once and can mean a great deal both to your correspondent and often to yourself.

Chapter Eight

APPLYING
FOR A JOB

When you write a letter applying for a job, you become a salesman, complete with product, sales presentation, and an order at the end. The product is yourself, the presentation is your letter, and the order you're seeking is an interview. Not a job: an interview.

Few jobs, if any, are gained by a letter, however good it might be; they follow a successful interview, which, although important, is outside the scope of this book. Before that you have to convince your prospective employer that he should see you rather than all the other applicants. And you do it by remembering something that most of the rest are going to forget.

They will be giving a great deal of thought to what they want to say, but you'll have a much more important question in mind as you write—and it is the only one that matters: *what results do I want?*

A friend of mine, the personnel manager of a large group of companies, received the following letter:

Further to your advertisement for a secretary-assistant to your Overseas Sales Manager, I wish to apply for the post.

I have always wanted to work for a big organisation like yours, as I like the opportunities for social contacts it brings and the chance to deal with people rather than things.

I studied French and German at school and still remember some of it. No doubt the job you are offering would help me to improve my languages. I would like that.

I can type accurately at 65 words per minute, but I would really prefer a position where typing is kept to a minimum, which is why I find the prospect of overseas travel attractive. While on that subject, perhaps I ought to mention that I have already booked a holiday in Benidorm for the last two weeks in July this year.

The young lady went on in much the same vein for another two pages, and my friend said that she'd told him just about everything except the time she liked her coffee served. She wasn't offered an interview, and that was a pity, because in all probability the job would have been right for her. She had been so concerned to tell the company all about herself that she'd forgotten her main aim: to make them want to see her.

Remember, you are trying to sell yourself in what is almost certainly a buyers' market; and to do this you must make your prospective customer (the employer) want to feel that he really can't overlook this bargain (you). So how do you do it?

It is safe to assume that the restrained approach is most likely to succeed. True, a potential employer might well notice a letter headed 'Special Offer—15% Off' or 'Free Diary with every Joe Bloggs engaged!' But I doubt whether this would have the effect on him that you want. And 'Buy Now—Pay Later' might create quite the wrong impression. No, all you need to do is to look at things from the employer's point of view and show him how what you have to offer is going to help him. If the young lady whose letter we've just read had written something like the following, my friend would probably have interviewed her. Her letter would have showed not

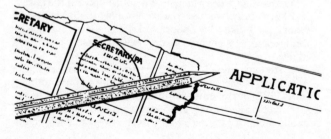

only that she had the right qualifications but also that she was concerned with what she could offer his firm.

> Your advertisement for a secretary-assistant to your Overseas Sales Manager was most interesting, and I would like to be considered for the post.
>
> I can type accurately at 65 words per minute and am also good at dealing with people. This must be an important part of the work, and I believe I would be able to bring more than ordinary secretarial skills to the job. Having studied French and German at school, I already know something of the languages and would work hard to learn more in order to help your Overseas Sales Manager.

She would have needed to go into more details of her experience and qualifications, of course, but you will see the pattern emerging. The emphasis is no longer on her but on what the company stands to gain by giving her the job. At this stage it would be foolish of her to introduce irrelevancies like already-arranged holidays; such things can be discussed at the interview, when they will almost certainly be raised by the employer.

Remember always that your letter of application is vitally important. Never send it off knowing that you could have written a better one and hoping to create a more favourable impression at your interview… because you won't be given the opportunity to bedazzle your prospective boss with your charm, skill and wit. He will be too busy seeing those applicants who have shown him by their letters that they are prepared to take that little extra trouble which he looks for in those whose wages he pays. And the chances will be that none of those attending the interviews are as highly experienced, as well qualified, or as able to do the work as you are. They just took a little more care in selling themselves when they applied.

Your first step is to find out as much about the employer and his business as you can. Clearly, it will not be possible if the advertisement is placed under a box number or through an agency, but in those circumstances no-one will expect you to have such information. If, however, as is most often the case, the advertisement gives the name and address of the company and the position held by the advertiser, this is your chance to make your letter of application more effective than those of most if not all of your competitors.

It always helps to be able to write directly to someone by name; think how much more impressed you are to receive a personal letter rather than one addressed 'Dear Sir' or, worse, 'Dear Sir/Madam'. So, if the name of the person to whom you are going to write is not given in the advertisement, it will be well worth a telephone call—even a long-distance one—to find it out. You need not explain on the telephone why you want to know his or her name. When the telephonist answers, something along the following lines will be perfectly satisfactory:

> Good morning. I wonder if you can help me. I need to write to your Works Manager [or whatever his position is] and want to make sure I have his name right. Will you tell me what it is, please?

When you're told his name, make sure before you ring off that you have the spelling right and also his initials. You won't help your application by only half doing the job, and you might make things much worse. I once misread an obscure signature, didn't bother to check it, and sent a letter to a Mr Hitler. (Well, there must have been more than one with that name.) When I called on the gentleman, I found to my consternation that his name was Flitterman and that he was, moreover, a leading member of the local Jewish community.

It is important that your letter is presented as neatly and in as businesslike a manner as possible. Occasionally, an advertisement will stipulate that applications must be handwritten. If this is the case, you can do no more than make sure that what you write is neat, properly set out, and legible. If you don't you will be wasting your time, because for some reason that employer considers it important that the person he or she engages is capable of writing clearly by hand.

If handwriting is not specified, however, you will create a much better impression if you type, or have typed, your letter of application. It goes without saying, of course, that if the job in any way involves typing you have an excellent chance of demonstrating the standard of your work, and you will be expected to make the most of it. But that brings us to another important point.

Your application might be one of several that you are sending out at the same time. If so, you could be tempted to duplicate your letter or even to have it printed, filling in the names of the employers as appropriate. Never, *ever,* do it. For one thing, it announces to your prospective boss that he is only one of many in your affections, and, being a normal sort of chap, he would much rather you considered him worth writing to individually. For another, it shows clearly that you haven't thought carefully about what you have to offer each employer, and you will recall that it's your ability to show each one what benefits you can bring *him* that is going to gain you your interview. This letter can decide your whole future. Common sense dictates that it would be foolish to try to cut corners with anything so vital. Better a few carefully-aimed rifle shots than firing off madly in all directions with a blunderbuss.

Unless you are one of the very few people who are able to write exactly the correct thing first time, it will be best if you make a preliminary rough draft. You can then make all the alterations you want before producing the final letter. You can be sure that, if you don't, you will find, just as you are about to seal the envelope, something you wish you hadn't said, or you'll remember something you have forgotten to include. And the temptation then to let it go will be far too great. Don't risk it.

Having prepared your draft and made all necessary amendments and additions, you're ready for the final step. Use good quality, plain, white paper, preferably of the standard A4 business size, and, whether you are

71

writing your letter by hand or by typewriter, make a carbon copy. This saves your having to remember what you wrote and will be helpful as a guide should you have to make other applications. Write on one side of the paper only, and, if it is necessary to use more than one sheet, number all pages after the first at the top.

Your letter should be as brief as possible consistent with setting out adequately what you have to offer. Remember that your object is to be invited to an interview, and it's neither necessary nor desirable for you to produce a combined autobiography and self-portrait.

Come to the point at once and stick to it. If you have a hobby that has given you experience or qualifications relevant to the job, then naturally you must mention it; you would be foolish not to. But an employer who is advertising for an industrial nurse or a toolsetter is not going to care much either way about your having played the lead in the local production of *Iolanthe* or possessing an international reputation as a breeder of budgerigars. He is, however, likely to regard such information in a letter of application as evidence that you aren't as efficient and businesslike as you want him to think. Take care, therefore, not to weaken your case by padding your letter with irrelevant details.

Unless the job is concerned specifically with religious, political, or trade union work, it is perhaps best not to mention at this stage that you are active in any of these fields. If, of course, your preliminary enquiries about the company have shown that the person you're dealing with shares your convictions and enthusiasm, and if the information is relevant to the post, it might be permissible to break this rule. But you must be very sure, and it is usually better to avoid introducing potentially controversial matters and thus possibly prejudicing your application.

If you have references, certificates, or diplomas from school, college, or previous employers, don't send them with your first letter, although it is worth mentioning that they are available. The same goes, of course, for specimens of your work, if such are relevant. In any event, these things are safer not sent through the post; there are too many stages at which they could go astray before they are returned to you. A better plan, if you have to send them later, is to send photocopies. Not only does this protect your originals; it enables you to send copies to a number of prospective employers at once. You can take the real thing along to the interview yourself.

When you have finished your letter check it thoroughly for mistakes. Errors in typing, spelling, and grammar *do* matter. Remember: for the present you're a salesman. Ask yourself whether *you* would want to buy a product that was battered around the edges or was shabbily presented. And what would be *your* reaction if it didn't quite work as it should and you were told to take it or leave it? Well, that's the reaction a prospective employer is equally justified in having when you offer him something less than he has a right to expect. You won't go far wrong if you try to see things from his point of view.

Be enthusiastic about your present and previous jobs, and don't give your reasons for leaving unless you are specifically asked to do so. Sometimes you *will* be asked for them; if you are, think carefully about what you say. It is perfectly acceptable to seek to better yourself by looking for more responsibility or a salary more in line with your ability. But employers do not take kindly to folk whose explanation for leaving is that they were overworked or that they had been passed over for promotion. This might well be true, but it equally might not, and nobody is going to risk engaging a slacker or someone who feels sorry for himself.

Above all, don't criticize your present or former employers. It's possible they ran a sweat shop and devoted their lives to defrauding the Inland Revenue, swindling their customers, and beating their wives. But they paid your wages, and loyalty is rightly regarded highly by all employers. The one you hope to work for could reasonably assume that if you are ready to disparage your former companies you might tell tales about him if all should not go well.

By now you should have a good idea of how to ensure that you will be one of the few applicants chosen for interview. Your letter will convince the advertiser that here is someone who can contribute something worthwhile to his business, and that he would be foolish not to see you. What you do when you get there will be up to you, but if you bear in mind the same principles as you did when you wrote your letter, you will have an excellent chance of securing the post. I wish you well.

If you are a school-leaver applying for your first job, you will be in a slightly different situation, in that you have no work experience to offer and almost certainly no professional qualifications. The same guiding rules apply, however. You must show your prospective employer that you can provide something he needs. Try to emphasize those points of your school career and outside interests which demonstrate that you have the qualities required to do the job. Membership of school societies or sports teams will show that you can work well with other people. Events you have organized at school or in connection with your hobbies will be evidence that you are able to use your initiative and have a talent for getting things done.

Be sure to list any examinations you may have passed, giving details of subjects taken and grades achieved. If you have studied any non-examination subjects relevant to the position you are seeking, it will help you to mention this, too. Similarly, if you've a certificate from your school or college testifying to the standard you have reached and to your character, it will be as well to include a photocopy with your application. A letter along the lines of that following is the sort of thing required. Notice the emphasis on 'you' and 'yours'.

APPLYING FOR A JOB

Telephone: Windlebury 1234

7 Elmwood Road
Windlebury
Dorset
AB1 2BC
21 June 19—

Mr I. Hiram
Personnel Manager
Allgoods Limited
1 High Street
Windlebury
Dorset
AB1 1AB

Dear Mr Hiram,

Your advertisement in this week's *Windlebury Bugle* for a sales assistant/trainee manager was most interesting, and I would like to be considered for the position.

Aged 16, I have just left school after taking "O" levels, in which I gained good passes in English, mathematics, commerce, book-keeping, and art. For the past year I have been a senior prefect at Windlebury comprehensive school and have been responsible for running the school bookshop during that time.

I was interested to read, in a recent trade review, of your plans to open a number of branches to meet the requirements of the two new towns being built to the south of Windlebury. I am keen to make my career in retailing, and during my last two school holidays I have worked in a supermarket, a department store and a gift shop, all in Blowston. I enjoyed the work very much, and feel that the experience I gained and my special subjects at school will enable me to bring something useful to the post you advertise.

You may find the enclosed copy of a testimonial from my headmaster helpful, and I would be pleased to give you the names of other people who have known me for some years and who will testify to my good character.

I could attend an interview at any time convenient to you, and I hope I may look forward to hearing from you.
Yours sincerely,
Leslie Selalott

Chapter Nine

US AND THEM: LETTERS TO THE AUTHORITIES

From time to time most of us have to write to government bodies or other official departments. As an experience, its joys rank about equal with those of a hole in your wellington, but the alternative is often either to suffer in silence or to run the risk of getting into trouble. So, given that the job has to be done, how do you set about it?

The first thing to do is *keep calm*. Remember that, while many of them appear to overlook it, civil servants are just that: paid servants of the State. And in a democracy you and I constitute the State...so that makes us their bosses. That doesn't mean, of course,

that we have an automatic right to suggest alternative filing systems for their sometimes unwelcome letters to us; the State in its wisdom has often given them authority so that they can carry out their duties properly. But it does imply that they are expected to deal with us courteously and they are not empowered to wield a big stick indiscriminately. So if you know you have right on your side, you need not worry, however fearsome the foe.

Summing up, then:

1 Keep calm.
2 Don't write anything until you have taken time to consider what you are going to say. Above all, never dash off a letter in the heat of indignation, worry, or just plain fury. You'll be sorry.
3 If you're in the wrong, don't try to wriggle out of it. Officialdom has a long nose, and you'd be surprised at what it can sniff out when it puts its mind to it. Far better to admit your sins, great or small, and concentrate on salvaging the situation.
4 *Never* be rude, however much you may feel like it, and whether or not the other person deserves it. You'll achieve far more by being polite, and, moreover, won't leave yourself open to later reprisals.
5 Be brief, consistent with stating all the relevant facts. Too much verbiage might mean that an important part of your letter is skipped over.
6 Be patient and, if necessary, persistent.
7 Keep a copy of what you write. You might need it.
8 As important a point as any: once you have considered your letter carefully, written it, and posted it...don't worry about it or its contents. You've done what you can for the present. Get on with something else. And besides, you'll look silly with your arm stuck in the mailbox, trying to get your letter back.

Your Member of Parliament
The only letter you're likely to receive from him will be

around election time, when he writes to remind you of all the good things he and his party have done and are going to do. He'll also, like nearly all politicians, demonstrate by expounding all the bad points of his opponents, his complete lack of skill in selling himself. Don't trouble to reply to this letter. You'll only confuse him if you do; he's sent the same one to every other house in the constituency.

You might, however, want to write to him from time to time, either to pass on your views about a particular issue, or to ask for his help in sorting out a problem. And fairness compels me to admit that whenever I have asked for help from my Member of Parliament, in whatever constituency I have been living at the time, it has always been willingly and promptly given, often in surprisingly generous measure.

It is worth remembering that he has access to a very wide range of help in all departments of government, and he will almost certainly know of sources you may never have thought of. You can always reach him at the House of Commons, London, SW1A 0AA, even during parliamentary recesses, for mail is forwarded to Members. Full details on how to address him are contained in Chapter Four.

> Can you help me, please? I am experiencing considerable delay in postal deliveries, and a seemingly endless stream of letters to my local Head Post Office has produced no noticeable improvement.
> I receive on average thirty letters a week, and a record kept during the past year has shown substantial delays in delivering at least ten per cent of them. First class mail often takes three or four days to reach me, and second class has, on occasion, taken up to ten days to arrive, with five days being usual.
> All delays have been reported to my local Head Postmaster and I believe him when he assures me that he is doing all he can to improve matters. It seems that much of the trouble stems from mis-sorting at the main office in Craston, eighty miles away. I wonder if you feel, as I do, that a system which sends mail a hundred and sixty miles

for sorting, when it is intended for an address only two miles away, seems less than sensible.

I shall be grateful for your help and will look forward to hearing from you in due course.

The Police

It is a criminal offence to waste police time, but that is no reason why you should hesitate to get in touch with them if you have good reason to do so. While it may from time to time seem fashionable for them to be criticized 'publicly—and there is the odd bad apple in every profession—they are almost always as helpful as anyone else. But remember that their job brings them into contact with the worst members of society, and they can not be blamed for a natural caution in dealing with people they don't know.

Most people's brushes with the law are perhaps confined to motoring offences, usually comparatively minor ones. And nothing hurts more than a parking ticket unfairly awarded. If you've a genuine excuse, it is worth trying to have it quashed...but be warned: don't try if you know in your heart you were wrong. And *don't* invent an excuse; they're all checked very thoroughly. Assuming you are well and truly on the side of the angels, however, write *immediately* to the Chief Superintendent at your local main police station. The senior officer there might not yet be a Chief Superintendent, but better to address him as that than as Sergeant.

Can you help me, please? [Notice how often it pays to begin a letter with this request. If you have any sort of a case, and the person to whom you're writing is at all reasonable, it puts you in with a chance.] I have today received the enclosed parking ticket in what you might think to be extenuating circumstances, and I would be glad if you could reconsider the penalty.

At 10.30 this morning I was driving along High Street, Anytown, when my small daughter, who was with me in the car, suddenly became ill. She lost consciousness, and I stopped the car outside Bloggs the Chemists, running inside to summon help and to telephone a doctor. I was in the

79

shop for no more than a minute or two, but when I returned to the car (in which I had left my handbag and shopping), the parking ticket had been affixed to the window.

I accept that by parking on a double yellow line I was committing an offence, although I was unaware of the restriction until I returned to my car. I am always most careful to observe traffic regulations, and this is the first time I have ever knowingly contravened one. But I feel sure you will understand that my concern for my daughter at that moment drove all other considerations from my mind. My only thought was to get help quickly.

My car was not illegally parked for more than five minutes and was moved to Bloggs's private yard as soon as the doctor arrived. As the incident occurred outside the rush hour, I do not think I caused any obstruction to traffic.

The staff at the chemist's would, I am sure, verify my account. I am very sorry for unwittingly breaking the law and would be most grateful if, in the exceptional circumstances, you could consider cancelling the ticket.

Inland Revenue or Customs and Excise

Contrary to what you might have heard, these government departments are staffed by men and women who, for the most part, are of normal parentage, have families who love them, and are kind to children and animals. And, to those readers who even now are muttering under their breath, 'Just like Himmler', I would reply that for every tax inspector who was earlier drummed out of the Gestapo for cruelty there are a hundred who genuinely will try to help...providing—and this is important—you are not trying to pull the wool over their eyes. And they can generally tell if you are.

Like the rest of us, revenue officers have a job to do, and we would be naïve if we denied that fact that some people are less than honest when it comes to paying the government what the law says it can expect. So we shouldn't be surprised if suspicion and a nose for detecting the not-quite-right are traits frequently seen in the make-up of both tax officers and customs personnel. It is, however, rare in my experience that if you have a genuine problem and nothing to hide they will refuse to help.

Whenever writing to your tax office it will help you and your correspondent if you can quote your file number. This is the number that appears on all of your tax returns, assessments, and demands. Don't worry, however, if you can't find it, but give as much information as you can to enable the office to trace your records: your employer's name and address, and your staff number, if you are employed, or your business name and address if you work for yourself. Similarly, a Value Added Tax enquiry to your local Customs and Excise office should show your VAT number if you are a registered trader. Such details make it easier for the staff to deal with your letter, and you can never harm your case by making things less troublesome for the other person.

> I think that for the past year I have been paying too much tax and would be glad of your help in checking my allowances and coding.
> My file number is 98/765332, and I work as a software developer for Marvel Micros Limited, whose head office is at Unit 1e, Hiteck Industrial Estate, Chipton. My staff number is 10101. I am enclosing my last P60 for your reference; if you need any other information from me, please let me know.

Public Services: Electricity, Gas, Telephone and Water

Correspondence with the public services is almost entirely concerned either with the quality or quantity of their service or with their charges. The quality of service varies from area to area and, people being what they are, from official to official. Sometimes it is surprisingly quick; at others you may wonder whether all life in their offices is extinct, a speculation which is invariably resolved next time a bill is due. This is where the quality of persistence comes into its own. One thing which is well worth bearing in mind is that any matter relating, even remotely, to safety is always dealt with promptly.

> Your records will show that I wrote to you on 3 April last, and again on 17 April, about my concern that the gas fire installed by you on 1 April was not working properly. In both letters I explained that the main tap appeared to be loose and that the appliance was not firmly fixed to the wall.
>
> You will not be surprised to learn that the tap has not tightened itself, nor is the fire fitting more closely to the wall. There is, however, a new development. My next-door neighbour tells me that during the past two weeks he has noticed a strange smell, especially early in the mornings. Moreover, my wife finds herself growing very drowsy when sitting watching television in the evenings.
>
> I am extremely concerned that there should be no leak of gas from my new fire, and would be glad if you would now treat the matter as urgent. I shall look forward to hearing from you, preferably in the form of a visit by your engineers, with no further delay.

Notice that you haven't actually said that your neighbour can smell gas, or, indeed, that his problem isn't caused by blocked drains or marital halitosis. And it's quite possible that your wife has always dozed off while watching television. But it's a fair bet that sometime during the next day she or you will be disturbed by the patter of gas board feet; they can afford to take no chances with safety, nor do they.

Insurance Companies

You may find it surprising that I should include insurance companies under the heading of 'Us and Them'. After all, don't their advertisements assure us that they stand firm round, under, and over us in all life's tribulations? Of course they do. And 99% of companies do just that 99% of the time, but it shouldn't be overlooked that they don't exist primarily to help us; they're there to make profit for their shareholders. What's more, almost all of them are vast, impersonal organizations ruled over by a powerful computer named KARG or something similar. Occasionally, one of our claims fails to fit in exactly with KARG's small print (he's always an unthinking monster), and he tells his human slaves to write us a 'Sorry, but...' letter. At such times, providing we have a genuine claim, the only way we can get what is due to us is to give KARG a kick in his silicon chips, for—make no mistake—when it comes to parting with his money he is very much one of Them.

The first thing he will know of your claim is when he receives the form you have sent in listing details of the accident. KARG understands nothing but forms. So when you receive your 'Sorry, but...', write the company a letter; that way a human will have to deal with it. Don't fire your first shot at the Chairman of what is probably a multi-million pound company, threatening to sue him for every penny they've got unless they pay up. The only result you will achieve is to make him dig his heels in and tell everyone else in the firm to do the same. Insurance companies know their legal rights, and they know yours, too. No, better by far to use a little common sense and courtesy; quite often in a marginal case a company, while not admitting liability, will make an *ex gratia* payment, feeling that the good will so gained is worth more than they are paying out.

> I have received your letter rejecting my claim for repairs to my bathroom shower unit because you consider that the terms of my policy do not cover accidental damage to showers.
>
> Your Houseowner's Comprehensive Policy has long been available; indeed, my own policy has been in force for fifteen years, during which time I have not made a claim. It seems to me likely that the wording was drawn up before showers became so widely used as they are now, and, like solar panels, they are not mentioned.
>
> I feel sure you will agree that showers are now comparatively common. You will know, too, that they are officially recommended as a way of saving energy. Because of this, it is possible you may feel they should indeed be included in the wording of your policy.
>
> It does seem that my claim is being rejected not because

it is unreasonable but because of what must surely be an unintentional omission from your policy. Will you, then, please reconsider the matter? I believe that the British Insurance Association would support my reasoning, but your reputation and integrity are so well known that I would naturally not write to them without first asking you to review it yourselves.

This letter has two points worth noting. You have let the insurance company know that, because you consider your claim eminently reasonable, you are prepared to refer it to the BIA, to which all the major companies belong. But you have shown them that you'd rather they dealt with it themselves. Equally important, you have worded your letter in such a way as to let them put things right without losing face. Never forget that if you want a person or a company to do something for you, you're more likely to get what you want if you make it easy for them.

Chapter Ten
COMPLAINTS

Complaining is an art in itself, and it is as important to know to whom you should write as it is to know what to write and how. Modern life is controlled by a vast network of people, organizations and authorities, all of whom seem hell-bent on imposing their wills on us unfairly. To deal with every possibility, or even most of them, would be impossible in a book of this size and scope, so we shall here confine ourselves to looking at ways of writing effective letters of complaint.

There are ten points you should always bear in mind when complaining. Failure to observe any one of them can result in needless work and worry, not only for the other person but also for yourself.

1 *Don't complain unless you have to.* Some people regard complaining almost as a way of life, finding fault where none exists. By all means protest if you have good reason to do so, but be sure that it is necessary. The known 'professional' complainer, whingeing needlessly about anything and everything, finds little sympathy when he really has something to complain about.

2 *Give the other person a chance to sort things out himself before you take matters further.* Wielding the big hammer to hit him over the head involves a great deal of effort and trouble. Opt for the easy way if you can.

3 *Complain to the right person.* Don't waste your time by complaining to someone who can't do anything about your problem. If the telephone number you are trying to ring is always engaged, there's not much point in swearing at the operator; find out who has left the receiver off at the other end; he's the one to blame.

4 *Know your rights.* Before making any complaint, especially one which might ultimately end in court or before the authorities, it is always as well to know what are your legal rights in the matter. If you have any doubts on this score, do make sure before taking any step which might possibly prejudice your case, waste your time or money, or make you look a fool.

5 *Be sure it is worth complaining.* In some cases, the only result you can expect from a successful complaint is a letter of apology. Or the person you complain about will be reprimanded and, one hopes, won't offend others as he has offended you. Such a result is fine if that's what you want, but don't always expect material gain.

6 *Complain in writing.* That way there will be no misunderstanding or argument about what you have or have not said and no excuse for the right person's not replying. Try to ensure that your letters are typed wherever possible; again, this doesn't give the other party the chance to say he couldn't read your writing...and it always appears more businesslike.

7 *Keep all correspondence and documents relating to your complaint, including copies of your own letters.* Receipts, accounts, quotations and the like may all be helpful in establishing your argument. If the other party asks to see them, send photocopies; originals can easily be mislaid, whether by accident or intent.

8 *Always be courteous.* Flying off the handle, whether in person or by letter, might make you feel better temporarily, but it won't help you get your complaint resolved. And never attack anyone's character or integrity; the laws on slander and libel make no allowances for provocation. Be firm and assured, but be polite. If the person to whom you're writing thinks of you as fair and reasonable, he is more likely to listen to you sympathetically. He won't if you appear rude and aggressive.

9 *Be patient.* Often a complaint will take a long time to investigate, especially if you are dealing with a large organization. Make allowances for this before you start to protest that your first complaint has been ignored. And don't complain at all unless you are prepared to stick at it until you have seen it through to the end.

10 *Say 'thank you'.* Few people who have had a complaint resolved take the trouble to write a final letter of appreciation; and yet that little extra courtesy goes a long way towards ensuring that the folk who have helped will be happy to do so again.

The following is a letter which was sent successfully to a supplier of oven-ready poultry. Only the names have been changed to protect the guilty.

I have uncovered your guilty secret, but before exposing all in the popular Press I would be grateful for your observations.

Enclosed you will find a polythene bag from one of your products which was bought by my wife from the Woppavalu Store at Flangeton last week, taken out of our freezer late on Saturday night, and cooked for lunch yesterday. After the initial cooking in the microwave oven, we noticed that one of the bird's wings was bright green, a sort of delicate shade which would have been quite fetching in curtains or even an apple, but which was a little off-putting in an alleged chicken. We hoped, though, that the short spell of browning in the ordinary oven would improve matters.

No such luck. Our bird was nicely browned, save for one wing which remained persistently bright green; and it was green right through, not just on the surface. Being a religious man, I did what the Good Book tells us to do: I cut off the offending part and cast it from me, into the garden, where the local gulls aren't so colour prejudiced.

You will be pleased to hear that all the family are well today and that, as far as I can tell, there are no seabirds suffering from botulism, salmonella poisoning, or diarrhoea. So it seems that no harm has been done. We are, however, concerned that the usual high standard of your products may be slipping, and I'm sure you'd rather we brought it to your notice than suffer in silence or complain to all and sundry without telling you first.

It could be, of course, that the bird was merely unripe and that a spell on the window-sill would have put things right; we must try that next time. But I suspect the truth is more sinister: I believe that in an attempt to cut costs you are no longer breeding chickens, and that the large lorries which pass my home every day bound for your local plant are just a front. What we bought was no chicken; chickens aren't green. But there *are* green birds, aren't there? I believe that what we were sold was either a well-developed budgie or a medium-sized parrot, and I'd welcome your comments on this public scandal before questions are raised in the House. (Well, they've been raised in this house.) Worse still, think of the agony if a certain public-spirited lady on television got her teeth into it. At any rate, please let me know what you think.

That letter produced a prompt reply expressing concern, an investigation into the problem (the gall bladder had burst during processing), and a refund sufficiently large to cover the cost of at least two replacement chickens. Honour was satisfied, a minor fault on the processing line was put right, and, for good measure, a helpful friendship was established between myself and the consumer relations department of the company concerned.

A writer friend of mine bought an expensive new electric lawnmower that she used for a little over a month before her work took her overseas for a year, during which time the mower was put into storage. Her house and garden were looked after by a neighbour in her absence, and the first time she took out her nearly-new mower was to trim an already short lawn. Her switching it on was accompanied by expensive noises, the smell of melting insulation, and a plume of smoke. The motor had burned out.

A letter to the suppliers brought the not-unexpected reply that, sorry as they were, the mower was out of warranty and she would have to pay for repairs, which would cost £75. My friend resisted the temptation to suggest various ways of disposing of her now-useless mower, and wrote to the manufacturers. She reasoned that, while a few pages of well-chosen and carefully-composed abuse would doubtless make her feel better, they wouldn't get her lawnmower repaired any more cheaply. So she wrote along the following lines. First she explained why the machine, although now thirteen months old, had been used only five times. Then she went on:

> I do appreciate that the machine is technically out of warranty and that in those circumstances I have no right to a free repair. I feel sure, however, that so reputable and well-known a company as yourselves will be concerned to learn of this sort of trouble occurring with one of your major products.
>
> The machine cost me almost exactly £100, and I managed just four successful mowings before it broke down. Even for the pleasure of using a Flitandhack mower, a cost of £25 per time is a little too expensive. I would be interested to know your observations on what is clearly a less-than-satisfactory state of affairs for both of us.

The company replied quickly. They pointed out that, while they had no obligation to put things right, if my friend would take the machine to their local service depot they would examine it. If things were as she described they would replace the motor free of charge. They were, and they did. As my friend said later, that letter took her half an hour to write and saved her a bill for £75 — hardly a bad rate of pay.

From time to time all of us have cause to complain about neighbours. In fact, relationships between neighbours can be such that almost anything can, given the right conditions and the wrong people, result in friction. You may have, as I once did, a close neighbour who is overly fond of rehearsing with the pop group for whom he plays drums; in itself not necessarily a bad thing, it can be better timed than the hours immediately before and after midnight. Or perhaps he insists on burning his garden rubbish every fine Sunday afternoon throughout the summer, at a time when you're intent on annoying him with your snoring.

Whatever the problems between neighbours, it is always best to sort them out, if possible, by a friendly discussion and an appeal to reason. Most people respond to this approach. Some, however, don't, and it becomes necessary to make things more formal, perhaps even to the point of asking the law to intervene, although this should always be a last recourse. Remember you've probably got to live near them for a long time. Assuming that your complaint is reasonable and, if need be, sustainable by law, the first step is to write them a letter of complaint, formally asking them to stop annoying you.

One of the most frequent causes of this kind of trouble is pets, either your own or other people's:

I have already spoken to you twice about your dog coming into my garden, but, although you have assured me you would stop it, he has been in again several times this week. Indeed only today my wife has had to remove him three times.

Quite apart from the damage the dog does to the flower borders, he frightens my children to the point where they are scared to play in their own garden. Even if they go out, however, they are constantly fouling themselves and the house with the mess which your dog brings in but doesn't bother to take away with him.

I have no wish to take stronger action, for I value your friendship and am sure that you, too, are equally anxious to remain on good terms. But I really cannot let things go on as they are. I would ask you, therefore, once more, to keep your dog under proper control, please, and see that he does not enter my property. If you don't, you will leave me no alternative but to seek legal redress, and I should regret that as much as you would yourself. I feel sure I can count on your co-operation.

You will, I hope, notice that all these letters, while seeking to have something put right, have a tone of sweet reasonableness. There might possibly come a time when you have to stand firm on the letter of the law, but you can lose nothing by being polite and reasonable. And, in the event of a complaint ending up in court, the fact that you're the one who has been calm, considerate and restrained will stand you in good stead.

One final point. At the beginning of this chapter I advised you not to complain unless you were prepared to see it through to the end. Naturally, legal action is always a last resort and is always expensive, whether or not you gain compensation at the end of it—not at all certain if the person or company you are suing has no means of paying you and the court. Some people know this and trade on it, making virtually a profession of taking advantage of the gullibility or good nature of others. So never threaten to use the law unless you are prepared to do it; and, having so threatened with no response, waste no more time before setting the wheels in motion. Such people regard magnanimity as weakness.

Chapter Eleven
LETTERS TO THE PRESS

Letters to the press should always be addressed: 'The Editor' and sent to the editorial address of the newspaper or magazine concerned. This may not always be the same as the address for advertisements, and it is sensible to check with a recent copy before writing. Since editors always receive more letters than they can possibly print, they can afford to be selective, and if you want yours to appear in his pages it pays to see things from his point of view.

He has limited space, more than sufficient letters to fill it, and, with many demands on his time, doesn't want to do more work than he has to. So make your letter short, to the point, and well-reasoned. Come to the point early, making it clear what you are writing about; and if your letter refers to something which has already appeared in the newspaper or magazine, refer to it as exactly as possible: give the title of the article or item and the date of the edition when it appeared.

Remember that the editor's job is to edit: if he feels he

ought to print your letter and it is too long or vague, he will cut out those parts he considers superfluous. It's just possible that in so doing he will remove something you feel is important; so it is clearly better that you should do your own editing before you post the letter, eliminating all needless words and detail.

Unless you know the editor to be a lady, begin 'Dear Sir' and end 'Yours faithfully'. If you need further information on this point, you will find it in the chapter dealing with starting and finishing your letter.

You can write to the press about almost anything you like, but most such letters fall into one of the following categories:

Suggestions or Statements of Opinion

As a lifelong resident of Puddlehampton, I feel it is about time that our town council banned the use of transistor radios on the beach. While accepting the right of people to listen to the radio if they wish, I believe equally strongly in the rights of those of us who prefer to spend our time by the sea in more private pursuits.

It is difficult to ask for a noisy radio to be turned down without giving offence, for the perpetrators of this nuisance are clearly, by nature, inconsiderate of the comfort and feelings of others.

Replies to Earlier Letters

I was interested to read in your edition of 13 June the letter from Mrs Ottoline McNurdle in which she advocated the banning of transistor radios from Puddlehampton beach.

While agreeing with her contention that individuals should not have to suffer the noise from transistor radios concealed behind the next windbreak, I feel she would have a stronger case were she to stop using the beach as a practice ground for her bagpipes every Sunday evening. My lady-friend and I find the sound most distracting, and, what is more, as she marches up and down she kicks sand over us and others similarly engaged.

Appeals for Information or Help

Newspapers can often provide the answers to questions not easily resolved by other means; if they are unable to deal with them personally, it is likely that they will be able to suggest other avenues of enquiry. They can, too, by publishing your appeal in their letters column, invite their readership to help.

> I am trying to trace an old friend whom I know to have lived in Twisleton a few years ago, and would be grateful for any help you or your readers can give.
>
> He is Canon Algernon Ball, and his address was once 3 Rose Cottages, Abbatoir Lane, Twisleton. He was, I believe, working as a gunnery instructor for the Church Army before being discharged, but they are unable to help me.

Letters Conveying Information

The scope for such letters is virtually limitless. They can range, for example, from a recipe which the writer thinks might interest other readers to a note about the origins of a national custom which has perhaps become topical. Items of local interest are always welcome.

> Readers may like to be reminded that next Tuesday is the forty-seventh anniversary of the introduction of the greater purple-spotted cobra to the woods on the west side of Deadman's Common. This snake is a native of the unpopulated areas of Northern Tibet and is widely thought to be a factor in controlling the spread of the slant-winged cassowary in those districts. As the cassowary is a distant relative of our own gruntlethrush, this might account for the absence of that bird in local woodland.

Letters of Complaint

These might deal with something that has appeared in the newspaper, whether editorial or in another reader's letter. Or they could refer to any other topic on which you feel particularly strongly.

> I read your article last week sympathising with the policeman who was crippled when attending a fire at the local comprehensive school, and feel I must protest most strongly at your biased reporting.
>
> The policeman concerned had only himself to blame. He should have realised that the seven teenagers he found inside the building at 11.30 p.m. that evening were public-spirited citizens who were trying to extinguish the

fire themselves with anything that lay to hand. It is a well-known fact that books, piled high enough, can put out a fire, and I for one am prepared to accept the youths' explanation that they had no choice but to keep the books in place with desks and a blackboard.

I am disgusted by this blatant abuse of police powers and the subsequent prejudiced conviction of these brave teenagers. After all, a fine of £5 is a lot for a nineteen-year-old to find. What is the world coming to when such harrassment of our young people is permitted?

Letters of Appreciation

Although not as frequent as they would like, such letters are always welcomed by editors.

I and my family send our thanks to you and your staff for your recent series of articles on advances in the treatment and rehabilitation of the disabled. My father is recovering from an industrial accident that resulted in his losing a leg, and an unpleasant side effect was the depression and sense of futility he has felt since the amputation. Your accounts of people who have overcome similar handicaps have done much to dispel his fears, and he is now looking forward keenly to an active and useful future.

or, perhaps:

This morning, while I was walking along the riverbank near Waterton, I saw a little girl fall into the water on the other side. A young man of, I should imagine, about seventeen and who was passing at the time dived in immediately. He had difficulty in reaching the child because of the fast current, but eventually he succeeded in getting her to the far bank, where two more passers-by helped them out of the water and returned the little girl to her mother.

Being on the opposite bank, I was unable to do anything myself, and was dismayed to see the young gentleman climb on to his motorcycle, dripping wet, and ride away before anyone could ask him his name. So far as I know, his identity is still unknown.

I was able, however, to make a note of the registration number of his motorcycle: AMN 123. In an age when young people are often criticized unfairly for their lack of social responsibility, I feel that this young man's courage and prompt action deserve mention and commendation, and I would be glad if you would help to ensure that his bravery does not go unnoticed.

Index